MELANIE BLAIKIE

TEACH WHAT YOU DO

THE HANDBOOK FOR TEACHING CREATIVE SKILLS

Dedication and Acknowledgements

This book has been years in the making. I didn't suddenly become a teacher or an author. It started when I first picked up a crayon and found it felt good to be creative.

I would like to thank my family for your endless encouragement on my creative journey and every single student who has ever attended one of my classes, your smiles and kind words of appreciation mean so much and were the inspiration for this book.

Also, to my wonderfully talented and resourceful creative friends. Meeting you has been just the best thing ever. Your support and friendship have changed my life – *thank you!*

CONTENTS

An Introduction from the Author

Firstly, thank you for buying this book. I already love the fact that you're really thinking about teaching what you do.

Now is a great time to get started on a new adventure teaching your own successful and profitable creative classes.

Right now, we are privileged to be a part of an amazing creative revolution. Arts and crafts, traditional and contemporary are capturing the imagination of a whole new audience. The rise of the slow food movement and artisan makers has rekindled a deep interest in process over mass production.

Consumerism is giving way to an appreciation of experience over possession as we seek more meaningful lives by nurturing our innate desire to do something useful with our hands.

We all know how fabulous it feels to take time out and learn something new. Creativity is catching and students of all ages and interests are now queuing up to get making. More importantly, a new wave of creative venues, hubs, clubs and craft schools are actively seeking confident and inspiring teachers – could this be you?

I'm guessing what you're missing right now is the real sense of this being something that is within your grasp? You might be intrigued by the possibility of teaching your own classes, excited by the idea of earning an income independent of your main career, and super keen to get started. Just not quite sure how?

I am convinced that now is the time to take a deep breath, and step up to the challenge of teaching what you do. It will be scary at times – sorry there's nothing I can do about that – but I am going to make it as easy as possible by helping you to understand the mechanics of the classroom and how to plan a knock-out lesson.

I'll be sharing tips on dealing with tricky situations and my secrets on looking confident, even when you don't feel it....!

Above all, I will do everything I can to help you believe this is something you CAN do. Because, at the end of the day, if you don't do it know you've bought this book, you can be sure that someone else will be brave enough to take the next step – and I'd hate them to take your place on this wonderful journey.

Let's get started ....

Melanie Blaikie

CHAPTER ONE

Looking at Motivation

'Fight for the fairy tale – it does exist'.

William Shakespeare

WHY DO I WANT TO TEACH AND WHY WILL PEOPLE COME TO MY CLASSES..?

Key learning points in this chapter

- Why now is the time to teach what you do
- What is a 'side-hustle'?
- The importance of understanding your own motivation for teaching
- Why you need to know your customer
- The world of creative classes is changing & why we need to adapt.

The Creative Revolution – it's happening now!

We are surrounded by a new generation of amazingly talented and inspirational creatives in fields as diverse as calligraphy to cheese making and sewing to social media skills. It's wonderful to think that we too, can be part of this amazing creative revolution that's happening all around us, right now.

Using your creative or artistic skills to earn an income is no longer seen as quirky or alternative. It gladdens my heart to see artisan makers and contemporary crafters making their way in the world with their beautiful products. The worldwide market is now on our doorstep, thanks to the internet and social media means we can showcase our talents to a whole new audience.

Or so it would seem... but the reality is that it is still a challenge to make ends meet relying solely on a creative income. Etsy, for example now has over two million active sellers and it can be incredibly difficult, not to mention disheartening, trying to get your products noticed. Fairs, festivals and makers markets too, can be a costly and time consuming business.

So, maybe now really is the time to consider alternative ways to earn by doing what you love?

So, what exactly is a 'side-hustle'?

A growing trend of recent years has been the rise of the creative 'side-hustle'.

The idea of a 'side-hustle' has been around for a while but for the UK audience this American terminology might be new. It could be translated as being a 'side-line', a way of earning an additional income alongside a regular salary.

Sadly, we continue to find ourselves under the pressure of rising property prices and less job security but surrounded by inspirational role models who have started a business in their garage or at their kitchen table and made it big. The question is; how to follow their lead and maximize opportunity with minimal risk. Many creative are discovering a 'side-hustle' is the answer, the chance to be an entrepreneur without giving up the day job – just yet.

By chance, this method of growing a business exactly mirrors my own experience. By necessity, I started a small business using my jewellery making skills and then transferred those skills into teaching others how to make jewellery.

The difference between these two closely related creative enterprises was startling. I was no longer working until midnight in my lonely workshop making things that might not sell. Instead, I advertised my classes and people signed up. My own creative side-hustle was born and I haven't looked back!

So …….

WHY DO I WANT TO TEACH?

This is such an exciting chapter to write. At the very beginning of any new venture lies a wonderful world of possibilities, full of new skills to teach, new people to meet, new challenges to rise to and new friends to make. It would be so easy to jump right in and start advertising those classes. But before we do, I want us to sit down together, grab a notebook and pen and take a few moments to consciously consider why we're doing this...

Exercise - Without thinking about it too much, jot down as many reasons as you can think of as to why you want to teach what you do?

Here are some common answers

- Seeking a more flexible lifestyle - If this is you, then working on your very own side-hustle could be the answer. Plan your classes around family commitments, your 'day job' or even your fabulous, exotic holidays and be the envy of your friends!

- I want to share my skills – if you love what you do then the opportunity to enthuse others to get creative can be incredibly satisfying.

- 'I've been to a class and it looks easy' – I suspect you had a very good teacher...! Leading a group through any practical exercise requires a huge amount of preparation and energy. It can be both exhausting and exhilarating. The real skill is to make it look effortless.

- 'I love being with people' – This is so important. Teaching is all about people. It is so much more than simply the communication of information. Working with people in any forum can be challenging but also inspiring and enlightening.

- Job satisfaction – I believe my teaching gives me a huge amount of job satisfaction. I love what I do but I'm very aware that different things make us happy. What suits me may not suit you. The teachers I know each have their own style of working, and their own personality which they bring to the role. Experiment with what suits you and make it your own.

- Money – Are you hoping to earn from your new ventures? Maybe it will be your sole income or to supplement existing finances?

Curiously, viewing this new venture as a means to make money often seems to be at the bottom of the list. Maybe it's because money is something we feel a bit embarrassed to talk about, but why?

From the very beginning I was adamant that if I was going to put in this amount of effort it had to be financially rewarding. So, throughout this book we are going to be business-like and plan for this to be not only enjoyable but also profitable.

'Working as a patisserie chef I found I really enjoyed training and mentoring, and gain tremendous satisfaction from seeing students learn and progress. I started to explore the possibility of teaching and realised it was the career I wanted to pursue. I've never looked back' Katie Churchard, Bake Off: The Professionals

Why is it important to think about our own motivation at the start of our journey?

Like any creative adventure, becoming a teacher will be full of surprises. Most of them will be happy experiences but there will inevitably be some that will make you question why you ever wanted to do this. There will be moments of exhilarating joy when everything goes well, but there will also be moments when you want to give up. There will be times that will challenge your self-confidence but lots more when this seems like the greatest job on earth. Every teacher I know experiences this range of emotions – sometimes all in one day!

To have deliberately decided why this new venture is important to you will be very helpful as we work through this book. Hopefully, the thoughts you have jotted down in the exercise on page 15, will help you to make wise and informed decisions to shape your new enterprise in the way that will be most meaningful to you.

'I'm a natural teacher as I love showing people how to do things for themselves, and I've been doing that most of my life. I've always intended to teach but only started last year, mostly because other stuff got in the way'. Sian Hamilton, editor Making Jewellery magazine.

WHY WILL PEOPLE COME TO MY CLASSES?

Before we start to plan any class, it is important to put ourselves into the shoes of our customer and think about what might motivate someone to spend time and money on one of your events. Only once we understand why students want to attend our class, can we set about making it a great experience for them. This section could be called 'understand your customer' and it's a really important exercise to undertake.

Exercise: jot down as many reasons as you can think of why people might want to sign up for your classes.

Here are some common answers

- To learn a new skill – Yes! Signing up for a class is a great way to get started with a new hands-on skill.

- To improve on an existing skill – This could be one step up from beginners or a master-class in a niche technique or process.

- The opportunity to be creative with guidance – Creative and practical skills are often easier to learn and engage with in a classroom setting with a real person on hand to answer any questions.

- Given the class as a voucher – In the drive for 'experiences over possessions', I've noticed a rise in classes being given as gifts for all kinds of celebrations.

- Just for a 'day out' – Why not? It's great that learning can also be a leisure activity. It's worth noting that for this type of attendee, achieving any kind of competence with the skills being taught may not be their primary motive!

- Special occasion such as a birthday or a hen party – Similar to gift vouchers. Events or experiences to mark special occasions are becoming more popular. Students will expect a fun experience as well as great creative take-aways.

- As the benefits of creativity to our physical and mental wellbeing are becoming more widely recognised, I've noticed an increase in people booking for respite or therapeutic reasons

In short, people will come to your classes for many different reasons. Some are very straight forward – wanting to learn a new skill, for example. Others can be more complex and may only become apparent much later.
Either way, we need to be very sensitive to motives for attending and build our classes to please our customers.

It's a simple concept and may sound obvious but it's so easy to get caught up in what we, as teachers want to talk about, it can easily be overlooked.

A new horizon for creative classes...

I've been teaching jewellery making skills for around ten years and there is a distinct change that I notice compared to when I started out. Signing up for a class is now a very socially acceptable way to spend your spare time. Similar to booking in to a spa or going to the cinema, a workshop, course or retreat is now seen as a relaxing, sociable, leisure activity with the added benefit of learning life-enriching skills. The mental, physical and social benefits of being creative are now widely recognised and promoted, which is great news. Rather than just signing up to master a skill, today's students aspire to be part of a more creative lifestyle and all that goes with it.

I mention this because it adds an interesting and important facet to the 'why will people come', discussion. I sense less emphasis is expected on technical mastery and more on delivering a sociable, entertaining, rewarding and fulfilling experience.

Of course, this won't apply to all of your classes or subjects. Almost all creative fields have some aspect where only applying the correct technical process will ensure success. But in today's busy world there are a rapidly growing number of potential students who will see this solely as an opportunity to relax and have fun.

ACTION POINTS FROM THIS CHAPTER

- Take time to identify and record your own reasons for wanting to teach. This will be invaluable later on.
- If you're venture will be a 'Side-hustle', consider how this will fit with any existing work commitments.
- Consider where financial reward sits in your personal set motives for teaching.
- Get to know your customer. Write down why you think people will come to your classes and how you will meet their expectations.
- Consider how you might adapt what you offer to appeal to a leisure-learning audience.

CHAPTER TWO

Personal Qualities

'People will forget what you said, people will forget what you did, but people will never forget how you make them feel'

Maya Angelou

GREAT TEACHERS – ARE THEY BORN OR MADE?

Key learning points in this chapter

- The mysterious art of being a great teacher
- The essential personal qualities you'll need to succeed
- Why passion and patience are vital for teaching
- How social media has changed our perception of learning

If this is the first time you've dipped your toes into the wonderful world of teaching what you do, be prepared for an incredible new experience. You will learn so much, not only about your subject and how to become a good teacher but most importantly, about yourself...

If you're reading this book I'm guessing it's because you don't consider yourself to be a teacher. You might be intrigued by the idea of teaching what you do but are not sure if you could. Or, you may already be thinking this could be the path for you and have bought this book as a guide. I'm going to share a secret with you here: I'm not really a teacher either. So, now we've got that out in the open, how is it that I'm writing now about how to teach?

For the record, my only previous experience of teaching was when I worked at the De Beers' training school in London. Here, new recruits to the world's largest diamond trading company were inducted into the mysterious and glamorous world of diamonds as they learned how to assess, grade and value the precious stones. I loved this work – to be honest who wouldn't and it left me with an appreciation of how satisfying it can be to share technical knowledge and teach a career-changing practical skill.

When the idea sprung into my head that I could teach jewellery making, I had very little experience of teaching a class and no concrete plan as to how to make it happen. I have a lifelong passion for and plenty of experience in the world of fine jewellery but I was embarking on a completely new journey into uncharted waters.

However, when I was considering the possibility of running my own classes, it felt a million miles away from the glossy office that had been my only previous 'classroom'. This time, I was doing it on my own, for myself, and my family, and it was much more daunting!

The tipping point came with the chance discovery of a new material that I believed would transform the silver jewellery making world. Pure Silver in a soft pliable, clay-like form, which could be easily worked, with very little need for specialist skill or technical knowledge.

It was a real game changer in my world and, at that point, very few people knew about it. I could immediately see the possibilities.

My original plan – to make and sell my own jewellery designs – suddenly took a back seat when compared to the possibilities I could imagine if I shared this wonderful discovery with other people. So, with a little knowledge and a huge amount of passion, I rewrote my plan and decided to teach.

Your own decision to teach your skill probably won't have been fired by the invention of a new creative medium. Or, maybe you have discovered a technique or a tool that deserves to be shared with the wider world. However, I think it's more likely that this is something you've been considering, maybe because you enjoy attending creative classes yourself, or have met one of the many truly inspiring creative instructors who already call this their 'day-job'. Or perhaps it's because you love meeting people and genuinely want to share your skills and knowledge.

Once I'd decided to pursue a career in teaching, one of the biggest challenges was finding employment that would enable me to make that change. I knew the type of course I wanted to teach and the audience I wanted to reach. I had to find a way to make it happen'. Katie Churchard, Great British Bake Off: The Professionals

I love meeting creative people and am constantly surprised at how many are considering teaching their special skills, but am also often disappointed at how few actively take up the challenge. The positive message here is: you are not alone if you find this a daunting prospect. Uniquely, in the world of teaching creative skills I find that very few of those standing at the front of the classroom are trained qualified, teachers. They may not have a formal qualification in teaching or even in the skills they are sharing but, like me, they have – at the very least – a real passion for their subject and from that passion stems the confidence to teach, share, inspire and encourage others to do the same.

'In the early days, my biggest challenge was my own self-confidence. But you quickly learn to listen to feedback from other people rather than the voices in your head – you have to, otherwise, you wouldn't succeed at anything'. Simon Sonsino, Director, Ardington School of Crafts

Over the last few years, social media has played a major part in fuelling our love for sharing knowledge. It is now easy to create really quite professional instructional videos using no more than just a mobile phone.

I find it fascinating how the world of teaching creative skills is being transformed with the spread of online learning. Now, it seems, almost anyone can make a short video on a mobile phone, upload it and quickly become an expert in any chosen field. You may have done this yourself? From icing a cake to eyebrow-shaping tips, the Internet is full of examples of ordinary people sharing their skills. And although some are definitely more informative than others, we still love watching them!

So, in the twenty first century does the key skill for becoming a teacher lie in being super-confident with a mobile phone? I think not. Teaching hasn't changed. Put simply, it is the exchange of information, from an individual who has it, to one who does not. Teacher to pupil. It is also interesting to think of information as a modern currency. If we have skills others want to learn they will almost certainly be prepared to pay to learn them.

But first of all, please think about someone in your life who has taught you something useful; how to change a password, wrap the perfect gift box or make ultimate cheese on toast...! What we're really talking about is someone who has been a good teacher. It might be important here to draw a distinction between formal and informal learning. A 'formal' teacher might be the sort you've met at school or university, but someone you've learned from 'informally' could be a work colleague, a neighbour or a relative.

In short, it's someone who wasn't being paid to teach you, but still had a useful skill they were happy to share. Very often, when I do this exercise with a group, the person who comes to mind is a close friend or family member. Surprisingly, the older generation now often talk about learning IT skills from their grandchildren!

Exercise: Think about someone who has helped you to learn new skills. Why did you enjoy learning with them? What positive qualities did they possess?

When asked to describe why this person was so successful at passing on their specific skill, words and phrases that commonly come to mind are:

- Patient – To teach we need to accept and understand that everyone learns at different speeds. As learners we dread the thought of being the only one who doesn't 'get' it. Remember how that feels and be prepared to cultivate endless patience…!
- Easy-going – if one explanation doesn't hit home, try another, demonstrate from a different angle, have a cup of tea and bit of a giggle and if none of those work, well…. does it really matter?
- Down to earth – You may be 'metaphorically' standing at the front of the class but being able to engage with people from all walks of life, on their level, is a skill to nurture.

- Inspiring – If you have real passion for your subject and a true desire to help others achieve the best they are capable of, you cannot fail to inspire your students.

In short, we are describing everything a great teacher should be, yet none of the people we were thinking about in that exercise would have considered themselves to be 'teachers'.

'I don't have any formal qualifications in teaching but I do have a degree in psychology, which has been useful in understanding group dynamics and the challenges students face as well as helping them overcome their own personal barriers to learning'. Jamie Chalmers, Mr X Stitch

When considering teaching as a 'side-hustle', it's often the sense of lacking a formal qualification that holds us back, and yet we can see how unnecessary it really is. (Clearly there are some classroom situations where being incredibly knowledgeable is mandatory and we'll look at this in a later chapter, 'Do I need to be an expert').

I've now taught hundreds of creative classes and have undoubtedly discovered personal qualities I didn't know I had or ever expected to use in my new career. The more I learn about myself and the mysterious art of being a great teacher, the more I move away from those traditional ideals of being a subject expert or master craftsman. The everyday challenges of inspiring students and creating a great learning environment are more likely to be achieved through:

- Passion for the subject
- Great communication skills
- Empathy and patience – lots of patience!
- Ability to make it FUN
- Great organising skills
- A real interest people
- Willingness to work really hard

Some of these attributes I can help you with and will talk about further later in this book – getting organised and ensuring everyone has a great experience, for example. I'm hoping that passion and patience are qualities you can already recognise in yourself – be honest here.

I'm not saying that it's impossible to be a great teacher if you don't have those qualities, but I do know that it will be much, much harder.

You may not yet be feeling entirely confident that you have what it takes to lead a class of students but don't worry, it's still early days and we've a long way to go together and I'm confident we're going to get there. Stick with me through the coming chapters and very soon you'll be ready to start planning your own successful and profitable creative classes.

ACTION POINTS FROM THIS CHAPTER

- Think about someone you've enjoyed learning with. What was it about them that made them a good tutor?
- Jot down the qualities you recognise in yourself that you might need to use in the classroom
- Are there some characteristics or habits that you'll need to work on – being organised, for example?
- How will you make your subject FUN ?
- Why not ask someone who knows you well if they feel you have the right qualities to teach what you do?

CHAPTER THREE

When and Where ?

'The two most important requirements for major success are – first being in the right place at the right time and second, doing something about it'

Ray Kroc

FINDING THE PERFECT TIME AND PLACE FOR YOUR CLASS

Key learning points in this chapter

- How to avoid work overwhelm
- The most financially rewarding days to teach
- The best teaching time to ensure return customers
- What you need to know before teaching at home
- Your checklist for hiring a creative venue

In the last chapter we thought about your own personal motivation for wanting to teach what you do and also why people will sign up for your classes. Now it's time to get down to the practicalities of planning your classes.

WHEN WILL YOU TEACH?

Once I had decided that teaching silver jewellery was the way forward, I pretty much advertised my first class without giving any real thought as to where this might lead or the effect the classes would have on my home life. I think I was imagining that it would all somehow fit together seamlessly and life would continue in much the same way as before but now, I would now have even more time for doing the things I loved like walking my dogs and weekends away because I was going to be working for myself....right?

When I 'Teach What You Do' as a face-to-face class, I love students enthusiasm and excitement as they talk about their new venture but it would seem I'm not alone in under-estimating how time-consuming working for yourself can be and just how much of your personal life it can take up.

Don't get me wrong, I absolutely love every second I get to spend with my students but if I'd have realised where those very first lessons were leading, I think I would have sat myself down and consciously thought through how I would organise my diary – especially once things got busier.

Dividing your diary into key teaching times...

In terms of organising classes, the week naturally divides into three parts

- Weekdays
- Evenings
- Weekends

(We could further divide our diaries into term-time and school holidays and school hours versus the nine to five working day but let's start here...)

Each part of the week has its own benefits and downsides and also, I've learned, a distinct customer group.

'My first experience of teaching was a big class at a well-respected venue with a reporter from the local press amongst the students. I remember feeling very nervous. I overheard one of the class comment upon how professional everything looked, which gave me confidence'. Louise Talbot, Cutting the Curd, Cheese making Classes

Let's start with Monday to Friday

Monday to Friday classes may seem the perfect fit if you have family you want to spend time with or a busy weekend social life in which case, I envy you and am waiting for my invite…..

If teaching what you do is a 'side-hustle' or an add-on to your day job, it may be possible to reduce hours in your main job and replace income with your classes – and still have weekends free!

However, I consistently find that there is less demand for weekday classes. Monday to Friday is the classic working week and unless your customer is super-keen and willing to book annual leave to attend your class, it may mean they pass over your event in preference to a weekend event.

Of course, there are a couple of notable customer groups who LOVE a weekday class. Parents or Carers of school age children might find they have more time to themselves during the week and positively relish the opportunity for some sociable, creative me-time whilst the kids are at school.

Another major group, well worth your consideration are people who no longer work and retirees. Often, young at heart, you'll find the older generation incredibly keen to learn new skills and sign up for new experiences.

If your classes lend themselves to either of the above groups, then it's quite possible that you'll have no trouble at all filling your dates. If you feel your subject is more suited to working age adults, it could be worth considering how you could engage with these 'weekday' customers as it will contribute to a more flexible future income.

Evenings

If your days are already busy, teaching in the evenings might work for you...? Best suited to short classes, evenings can be a great way to engage with a mixed crowd and create maybe an ongoing programme or a six week course, for example, that will build on skills and create a pool of returning customers. Just remember - this potentially could mean a very long day for you.

Weekends

I've put weekends last on my list because Saturday and Sunday are, without doubt, the most popular days for classes. When I was planning my new teaching venture, I remember thinking that although I didn't mind working the occasional weekend, I was secretly hoping this new lifestyle would be funding weekends in Rome / Paris / Barcelona (insert destination of choice). And interestingly, when I meet new Teach What You Do students, not working weekends is a common aspiration!

Of course, this new venture is completely under your control, that's the beauty of a 'side-hustle', it's your thing to do exactly what you want with. If you have no intention of ever working at the weekend that's absolutely fine, but please consider weekends have the greatest earning potential and you will need to work even harder if you discount them completely.

Weekend classes consistently fill best and are still the main source of my teaching income. Of course, I don't work every weekend and actively plan my year in advance to be at home for family birthdays, anniversaries and special occasions but it does mean I sometimes miss parties, weddings and other social gatherings because of work.

As much as I love my classes, my feet do drag a little when I know I'm missing an important social event or seeing my lovely friends. But this is my choice.

So, here is the difficult question I pose to you now. Do you want to work at weekends? If so, will that be every weekend or say, just once a month? Also, once you've made that choice, what would it take for you step outside of that boundary? For example, if you could earn four or five times as much by working one Saturday (Oh happy day...!!!) compared to that number of weekdays – would you accept? Be honest with yourself, this exercise is all about confronting those tricky decisions that will actually make life easier later on.

Of course, every situation needs to be evaluated on its own merit and this may not be of prime importance to you right now but it is something you should be thinking about.

WHERE WILL I TEACH?

The space you call your classroom may be dictated by the subject you plan to teach. Food related topics, for example, such as cheese making or cake decorating need very specific environments not only in terms of the equipment but also to comply with food hygiene regulations and health and safety issues. In this chapter I am going to concentrate on non-food subjects, but if your plan is to teach in this sector, you will need to take industry-specific advice before starting out.

'I mostly teach patisserie which requires very specific kitchen facilities. This limits where I can teach. For each class, I also need to check in advance that equipment and conditions will meet the needs of the techniques I'll be teaching'. Katie Churchard, Bake-Off: The Professionals

Teaching at home

For many new teachers, working at home is both appealing, convenient and can be very cost effective. So let's look at some of the essentials you'll need to think about before you teach at home.

(This list is only intended to act as a guideline for issues you may need to consider. I would highly recommend taking specialist advice before undertaking any kind of business activities from your home.)

- Suitable space or workroom

Clearly if you intend to invite people into your home to learn with you, you must have a suitable space that can easily accommodate your maximum number of students. You'll also need to ensure you have suitable chairs, tables or workbenches plus access to water and electricity if needed. Toilets - a downstairs loo is ideal here as who wants even the nicest students wandering around the house?

- Transport or Parking

How will students reach your house? Are there easy public transport links or if coming by car do you have access to sufficient, suitable parking areas?

- Household Insurance

Before you invite students into your home, check with your household insurance company as you may need additional cover.

- Landlord / Mortgage Company

Do check through any tenancy or mortgage agreements to see if they specifically mention or forbid undertaking any kind of business activities from your property.

- Public Liability

Public liability Insurance protects you against claims of personal injury or property damage that a third party suffers (or claims to have suffered) as a result of your business activities. Most insurance companies will be happy to help you with Public Liability cover and for a relatively small sum, it's worth the peace of mind. Don't assume that everyone will be as honest and understanding as you should something go wrong.

- Neighbours

Please be considerate to your neighbours. If your classes result in a noticeable increase in visitors to your property, cars parking in the street, more noise, rubbish or any general inconvenience for your neighbours they may have cause to complain.

- Food Hygiene

If you intend to offer and food or refreshments to your customers, check with your local Environmental Health team for any regulations or legal requirements. You might want to consider a Food Hygiene Certificate.

- Homely Surroundings

Apart from being convenient for you, working at home can generate a relaxed and welcoming vibe for your students. Fresh flowers, good coffee and maybe even some quiet background music while you work all adds to the ambience.

'It was discovering the perfect spot for a studio that prompted me to start teaching my photography classes. Here at Pin Mill in Suffolk, on the banks of the River Deben, we have wonderful light and picturesque surroundings with the added benefit of a fantastic pub right next door where we convene for lunch and more photography chat…!'. Anthony Cullen, Photographer

Hiring a Room / Hall / External Venue

If teaching at home isn't viable or just something you'd prefer not to do another option might be to hire a venue for your class. If possible – and sometimes it isn't – I highly recommend visiting the venue in advance and checking these points;

- Costs & Timings

Clearly you'll need to know the hourly or daily rate for hire but also check whether this includes time to set up and pack away at the end of the day or any other restrictions.

- Facilities

Check whether heating, lighting and use of tables, chairs, kitchen facilities are included in the price. Also check out toilets and parking arrangements, for yourself and students. Is there is disabled access and a suitable unloading area if you plan to bring your own equipment and tools etc.

- Public Liability

Check with the owner / organiser if they have public liability insurance that will cover you working on their premises of if you will need your own cover – see page 37.

Teaching by Invitation

A slightly different situation; this is where you are teaching by arrangement at an external venue which could be a college, craft school or creative venue, as their guest. You may have approached the venue yourself or have been invited by them.

Either way, your check list will be much the same as above. Although these types of spaces tend to be set up specifically for creative classes so facilities and equipment etc are often much better.

Wherever you teach you'll need to think about;

- Numbers

Are there a maximum number of students allowed at the venue or a minimum number below which the class becomes financially unviable, for yourself or the venue?

- Food and refreshments

If you are not providing these yourself, will students be able to make a hot drink or buy their lunch? If not, don't forget to include a reminder to bring a packed lunch in the booking information.

- Travel and Transport

Unless the venue is particularly well know, or easy to find it's a good idea to include the postcode and travel / parking options with booking information. This can save a lot of time and stress on the day....!

- Security

Do think about the security of your own tools, equipment and possessions and those of your students. Is there public access to your work area? Can the door be locked if you all leave the classroom, at lunchtime, for example?

- DBS checks

The Disclosure and Barring Service (DBS) helps to prevent unsuitable people from working with vulnerable groups, including children. If you plan to work with any of these groups do check whether a DBS check is needed. Even if it isn't a necessity it can still be good thing to have.

ACTION POINTS FROM THIS CHAPTER

- Consider your existing work/life commitments and identify the best possible times for you to teach.
- If you're thinking of working from home, make a list of the people or organisations you need to contact and start drafting contact emails.
- If working at home is not for you. Identify some potential local venues and contact them or visit.
- Design a paper or online checklist for your chosen class venue. It's great to be able to tick off tasks as you complete them!
- Be aware of any specific industry regulations or best practice that may apply.

CHAPTER FOUR

Lesson Planning

'A leader takes people where they want to go. A great leader takes people where they don't want to go, but ought to be'

Rosalynn Carter

CREATING THE PERFECT LESSON PLAN

Key learning points in this chapter

- Why you must have a lesson plan
- Why your lesson is not about what YOU want to teach
- How to still win when things go wrong
- The real reason why you must always encourage questions in class
- The two golden moments in every class which you mustn't miss

The foundation of any successful class is a sound lesson plan. The best teachers I know spend many hours honing their plans to perfectly meet their students' needs and expectations. But creating the perfect plan doesn't need to be complicated ….

The first time I welcomed a group of fee-paying students just happened to be an evening class. The advertised timings were 7.00pm – 9.30pm. Unfortunately, I can very clearly remember that at 10.30pm we were still struggling to get the project finished. It was an embarrassing and stressful situation where I felt totally out of control of the pace and the progress of the session. The students, not surprisingly were confused and uncomfortable with my seeming inability to work to the timings they expected.

This whole situation was so traumatic, that once I'd recovered – which took several days – I knew I had to examine what had gone wrong and do it better next time.

As previously mentioned, my route to becoming a teacher has been somewhat 'informal'. I started with great passion for my subject and very little understanding of the practicalities of running a class. On that evening, I remember feeling nervous when the students arrived but crossed my fingers, said a little prayer and felt confident that I could wow them with my enthusiasm and creative skills – what could possibly go wrong?

If I could speak to those students again, I'm sure they would agree that I provided them with a memorable evening but, unfortunately, for all the wrong reasons!

Looking back, the positive side to this experience was that it taught me the importance of lesson planning. I'd seen how easily time can run away, especially once I become engrossed in my subject. I knew I had to have a plan to keep me on track and prevent this happening again.

WHY A LESSON PLAN IS VITAL

- It will force you to think your class through – in detail
- It will give direction and purpose to your lesson
- It will save you time and stress later on
- It will contribute greatly to the smooth and seamless flow of your class – and who doesn't want that?

I love meeting new teachers and helping them get started on a new career. We talk about all the aspects of sharing creative skills that I've covered in this book. However, without fail, the very words 'Lesson Planning' are meet with a groan and - 'Do I really have to do this?' - 'I don't know where to start!'

My first lesson plans were pretty simple. A few timings sketched out a piece of paper, which I kept by my side. Over time, they have become more and more detailed. I confess to now being slightly obsessed with committing key learning points, progress checks, reminders and timescales, to paper. I find the whole process of thinking through each part of the day enormously helpful and produce detailed documents, which then become my blue-print for each class.

'I spend a minimum of two days planning each course I deliver – sometimes much longer. In class, I always have a pencil ready to adjust the lesson plan to meet the needs of the class'. Katie Churchard, Bake Off: The Professionals

If you are a creative person you will understand the concept of 'flow', of being in the moment, letting inspiration and the creative energy take you where it will. Doesn't this also apply to leading a creative session? Would it not stifle the creative expression of the learners to have things, well, too organised and rigid? It can be oh-so-tempting to take this view but the real beauty of creating a lesson plan is that it forces you to think though what you're doing – in detail.

Let's think of this in a different way. Imagine setting out on a journey you haven't made before. You know your departure point and eventual destination. With this knowledge, most of us would consult a map, google or set the sat-nav to fill in the missing detail – times, directions, potential delays or problems and the all-important ETA.

To start your class without a lesson plan is like setting off on that journey with absolutely no knowledge of where you're heading.
You know where you're starting and where you want to end up but that bit in the middle is left completely to chance. Just imagine what could happen. At best, you might be lucky and arrive at your destination by guesswork and at worse you could be floundering around for hours, completely lost. This latter is incredibly stressful – please don't do it to yourself!

I hope by now, I have convinced you of the importance of lesson planning but remember it doesn't need to be complicated. In the beginning, I hope you will be teaching relatively short classes – not more than one full day – in a subject you feel confident and comfortable with.

'I spend hours planning and preparing for each lesson. My courses are constantly evolving as I discover new and exciting techniques'. May Martin, Judge, The Great British Sewing Bee.

WHAT MAKES A GREAT LESSON PLAN?

Every confidently delivered learning experience consists of three key elements;

1. CONTENT – shaped by the aims and objectives of your class
2. TIMINGS – to maintain a comfortable pace and flow, for you and your students.
3. PRACTICE – fine-tuning the details

1. CONTENT
Planning for learning not planning to teach

By now, you may have a project or technique in mind that could be a good subject for your first class. We all have a favourite design or signature piece that would seem an obvious place to start.
But before you start planning the class *YOU want to teach* it's important to be ensure you are planning something your customers *want to learn.*

To do this, we need to briefly revisit chapter one where we considered what motivates people to attend a class. We discovered those reasons can be varied and not always obvious;

- To learn the basics of a new skill
- To add to existing knowledge
- To go home with a finished piece that will impress their friends
- Spend social time with friends or make new ones
- Needing some time out

If we can anticipate why students have signed up and what sort of class they are expecting it will help enormously in planning content that will meet their needs and make them happy. Are they a specialist interest group with good existing technical knowledge, for example, or a hen party just wanting a fun, creative session? We all want happy customers so we must understand their reasons for attending the class and have planned our content around them.

'It's hard to remember how long I spent getting the class planned originally but it was probably a couple of days. I have recently taught a few advanced days and they take about a day to put together, though the ideas may take months to come to fruition'. Sian Hamilton, Editor, Making Jewellery magazine

Exercise: Thinking about your potential customers, write down some ideas in the box for lesson content you think would make them happy. Doesn't have to be anything too polished at the moment, just ideas.

What Do Your Students Want To Learn?

I'm encouraging you to start simple, so planning a class where the objective is 'to learn the basics of a new skill' is good place to begin. This level of class should be easy for you to plan and anticipate projected timings.

To Learn the Basics of a New Skill

- These students have no knowledge at all of your subject
- They want to leave feeling confident with a few basic techniques or easy processes.
- If these can be combined into a small finished project it will consolidate learning. They'll leave with something they feel proud of, show their friends and be a good advertisement for your class!

I've seen some really fun and popular classes based around very simple techniques. The focus of these classes was not so much to teach a new skill that students would continue with and build upon, but to give everyone a fun and sociable evening out with some great creative takeaways.

Finished pieces with a real wow-factor always go down well here. It's hugely satisfying to see beginners exceed their own creative expectations and leave with a huge smile on their face, promising to return for a second class.

So, early on, you'll need to consider if the aim of your class if will be to learn beginner level skills and how those skills will contribute to a finished project. Create your lesson plan to achieve those objectives and you're on your way to your first successful class.

IMPORTANT: Do take every opportunity to chat with your students about their own creative experiences, interests and ambitions. These conversations will help you to become skilled in understanding what your customer is keen to learn and those important, underlying reasons as to why they have come to your class.

'My first class went really well. I know my teaching has improved since then but it still ran smoothly. I took my neighbour (a good friend) with me who joined the class. The day after, she gave me feedback both positive and not! This was really helpful; she's not creative and knew nothing about making jewellery so it was good to hear what she thought. I did change a few things afterwards as a result of her comments'. Sian Hamilton, editor Making Jewellery magazine

Explanation Is Everything!

I know that, in the beginning, I talked my students through the tasks, carefully explaining exactly how I did it. I can remember being quite surprised that although I thought I'd explained the process incredibly clearly, a few just didn't 'get it'. By encouraging students to ask questions at every stage, you will soon begin to appreciate what they find unclear and areas where your explanations are lacking in clarity.

'As a tutor you must be prepared to explain things many times over and in different ways. Repeat, repeat, repeat. I always say that there is no such thing as a stupid question!' May Martin, Judge, Great British Sewing Bee

Over the years, my ambition has always been for 100% of my students to understand me clearly and completely 100% of the time. I must say I haven't got there yet. I'm still aiming for the perfect explanation so I tend to slightly adjust my words for each class, dependent upon the questions asked by the previous class. I'm always learning from my students, always tweaking those descriptions and still aiming for that 100%.

There will always be those completely off the wall questions that leave me wondering if I really have been speaking a foreign language all along (!) but all teachers get those and they can be a truly enlightening insight to the minds of your students and how they learn. I find this aspect of teaching completely fascinating.

2. TIMINGS

Once you have a rough outline of the content of your class, it's time to start allocating some proposed timescales to the various tasks.

In the early days, this can really only be your best guess but after even one lesson you'll have a much clearer idea of whether you're on the right lines or need to make adjustments.

So, firstly, break the class down into broad sections

• Introduction
• Demonstration – technique 1
• Practice session
• Coffee break
• Demonstrate technique 2
• Practice session
• Thanks and End

You will know, roughly speaking, how long it would take you to complete your demonstration task. Don't forget you are well practiced and it will almost certainly take students much longer. We all learn in different ways and at different speeds so allow time for questions, re-caps or the need to repeat the demo.

'One of the most important tips I can give is that everyone learns at a different rate. What takes me five minutes to make will take students half a day. Patience is key, if you don't have patience don't teach'. Sian Hamilton, Editor, Making Jewellery magazine

Exercise: Think about the steps within one of your favourite projects. How long do they take you to complete? How long might they take you do demonstrate? Start to consciously allocate timings to common tasks.

Putting It into Practice

So, when thinking about timings, start with the immovables: the class start time, the end time and any planned breaks.

Within this structure, break your session down into shorter sections with projected timings. Sometimes, I plan sections of one hour or thirty minutes but more and more I find myself being very disciplined and sometimes even break sessions down into 15 minute blocks. This is especially useful for short classes of say, less than three hours.

Here is an example of a very simple plan I created recently for a beginner's class lasting 2.5 hours.

10.00 Introductions

10.15 Demonstrate Project and answer questions

10.30 Students work with silver

10.45 Check progress and advise 15 minutes work time remaining

(Note: Turn kiln on)

11.00 Drying time

11.00 – 11.30 Coffee

11.30 Put students work into kiln while I talk about firing

11.45 Work out of kiln

12.00 Polishing

12.15 Add fixings to finished work

12.30 Thank you and goodbye

Exercise - Create a lesson Plan

1. Choose a subject for your class based on skills your customers want to learn
2. Start with the 'immoveables', start, end and break times.
3. Break subject into smaller sections, plan demo's, time for questions and student practice
4. Allocate proposed timings
5. Add notes for self / action points / reminders

Best Laid Plans...

The real beauty of a detailed lesson plan is that with it by your side, you will very quickly know if things are NOT going to plan. **This is important.** If you know that a section you anticipated would take 10 minutes has in practice taken 20 minutes, it means you are in a position to do something about it. Can you shorten a planned break? Simplify the next section or leave something out that will help you to get back on track?

'At my first workshop, I'd underestimated how sleepy everyone feels after lunch. Consequently, we covered the content I'd planned to last an hour in just ten minutes. I've since learned that coffee, a good stretch and some fresh air re-invigorates everyone!' Jamie Chalmers, Mr X Stitch.

All classes are different, groups and individuals work at different speeds so it's important to recognise that rarely will your class progress exactly as you expect. Your lesson plan is not written in stone. Keep a pencil handy and be prepared to adjust content and timings to the needs of the group, as you go along.

I've become quite savvy to this unpredictable nature of timings so always keep a couple of tricks up my sleeve. If I find we're getting through the lesson more quickly than anticipated I'll add in an extra demo or short project to fill the space. If we're falling behind, I'll combine a demo and coffee break to save time or just talk less. (Yes, I know I do tend to talk a bit too much!)

My lesson plan helps me to feel confident, in control and prepared to enjoy the class. This means a better experience for my students.

Lesson Planning – Do It.

3.   PRACTICE

Practice Makes Perfect

Being able to control the flow, pace and timings of your class becomes easier with practice but if you're starting from scratch, how you can gain this all important experience?

To begin with, why not practice on your friends and family? They're usually on your side, can give you valuable feedback and working with them will allow you to check your timings. Alternatively, why not advertise a discounted class and explain that you're preparing to teach and need reviews for your website?

'I can't remember my first class. I can only remember that it went well and without hitches. But I had put in a lot of effort in advance in planning and preparation. I know the lesson plan was important so I spent time on content and timings and practiced with a group of friends beforehand.' Anthony Cullen, Photographer.

The Two Golden Moments of Every Class

My experience of teaching has highlighted two important moments in every class which I now feel if handled insensitively can make or break the students confidence in me as a teacher.

The first is that golden moment at the very beginning of each class – the Introduction. A confident, smiley, welcoming introduction to the class, to the venue and to yourself may only take a minute or two but its positive effect will be invaluable throughout the day. Plan what you're going to say, make eye contact and tell everyone they're in for a great time!

The second 'golden' moment is at the very end of each class. I've so often attended classes where students either drift away unnoticed or stand around unsure as to whether the class has finished or not. Be bold. A few minutes before the planned end time, make a point of getting everyone's attention, thank them for coming and praise their work. Most importantly, if the class has gone well and they have enjoyed their time with you, tell them what to do next. This is your opportunity to advertise future classes, excite them about learning more with you and don't forget to tell them how to book their next class, find out more or simply follow you on social media.

Collecting Feedback

The end of your class is a great time to collect feedback. Hopefully, you have a group of delighted students who will be more than happy to share their thoughts, comments and suggestions. These can be invaluable in helping you to shape and improve future classes. A short questionnaire to hand out and collect back once completed, is often the best way to do this.

Complimentary comments can be great to add to your website or use in promotional materials, provided you get the authors permission. A quick check box on the same form covers this off.

- Limit feedback to just three or four key questions
- Be sure to collect before students go home. Once they leave your classroom they will be far less likely to engage with your request.
- Read every comment and take note of any useful suggestions – there's always room for improvement!

'In my head, my first few classes were dreadful – riddled with mistakes but the feedback from students was very encouraging. That's why feedback forms are so important. It's the only way you can find out what you need to change to make it a better learning experience'. Simon Sonsino, Director Ardington School of Crafts

ACTION POINTS FROM THIS CHAPTER

- Start thinking about what your customer wants to learn not what you want to teach.
- Use the template to start planning your first lesson. Decide on content & consider the timings.
- Think about opportunities to practice your lesson before your first 'official' class.
- Identify a contingency project or demo that could fill an extra 10 minutes if needed.
- Draft your class Introduction & 'Outro'. What will you say?

CHAPTER FIVE

Becoming a confident teacher - it's all about you !

'The quickest way to acquire confidence is to do exactly what you are afraid to do!'

Unknown

THE ELUSIVE INGREDIENT – CONFIDENCE!

Key learning points in this chapter

- How to look confident even when you don't feel it
- Simple tricks to steady the nerves
- Why it's important to keep breathing…!
- Why you are what you wear
- How personal presentation can promote your brand

Confidence is an elusive ingredient in life. We all want to be confident, especially in front of our class. But how best to achieve that intangible state of self-assuredness is difficult to define.

This chapter looks at why you will almost certainly feel nervous before your class and what you can do about it.

Teaching your first class will be like anything else in life that you're doing for the first time. First day at a new job, first time driving a car on your own or meeting your prospective in-laws for the first time...!

Doing anything big that you've never done before, is always a bit scary and of course, you're bound to feel nervous. The important thing is not to let those nerves get the better of you ...... but how?

1 Preparation

If there's only one thing you take away from this book, I hope it will be the importance of being thoroughly prepared before you step into your classroom. This means

- You have thought through and understood what your students want to learn - not just what you want to teach them.

- You have created a lesson plan to meet those objectives

- Content and timings have been thoroughly worked through.

- You have tested the above on a practice run at least once.

- You have a standby project or demo up your sleeve, ready to pull out if you get through the planned content more quickly than expected.

- You have a spare set of notes and / or project materials ready to go if an extra student arrives unexpectedly.

- You've allowed plenty of time for travel and setting up so you're ready and relaxed when the first student arrives.

Knowing that you have worked through every one of these steps will provide you with the peace of mind that everything that can be prepared for in advance has been covered.

This in turn creates a sense of quiet confidence, you've done the very best you can to deliver the best possible class. You should be able to relax and enjoy this creative journey with your students.

2 Keep breathing

Something I often remind my students to do....!

It may sound obvious, we breathe, all day, without even thinking about it. But have you ever noticed how once you start to feel even a tiny bit stressed, each breath becomes quicker and shallower? At worst - and this often happens when we're concentrating really hard – we hold our breath completely, and actually stop breathing for a few seconds.

So, taking a minute or two before the class begins to be conscious of breathing deeply and calmly, really does work in helping to still the nerves. I do this all the time, and thoroughly recommend it.

Exercise – Mindful Breathing.

Take a moment whilst you are reading and feeling relaxed to notice how you are breathing.

Practice mindful breathing for a few minutes, think about expanding your lungs to capacity with each breathe - taking note of how it makes you feel.

Imagine yourself at the front of your class, and consciously try to maintain this relaxed, even breathe pattern.

3 Positive thinking

Create a mental picture of your class going really well, with lots of happy students, smiling and really enjoying learning with you.

Imagine them at the end of the class thanking you warmly promising to return and learn more. Believing you can do it and being able to picture yourself looking confident and happy in front of your class is a big step towards making it happen in reality.

4 Act Confident

This one is not so easy, but interestingly, our brains are easily fooled into believing what our actions convey.

If you stand tall, smile and breathe calmly, something amazing happens - you really do start to feel more confident. Act the way you want to feel. Most of the time, no one will notice you're acting......!!!

These tricks will help enormously in overcoming that crushing sense of blind panic that can so quickly engulf the unprepared.

Your hands are clammy, your heart is beating faster than a drum and at the vital moment, your mind goes completely blank. If you let this happen, no-one will enjoy your class – least of all yourself.

Interestingly, when I was interviewing the other teachers and tutors who have kindly contributed their thoughts towards this book, I was interested to know whether they still feel nervous.

These people are very experienced teachers who have been sharing their knowledge for many years. I was surprised that almost every one of them said that, yes, at some moments they do still feel that fear. However, what I went on to discover is that the nature of that nervousness shifts.

Whereas, at the start of their career, delivering a class to a dozen people would have been challenging, they now find it's speaking to a room of several hundred people that set the nerves off. Or, doing something for the first time, like delivering a technical new class or advanced programme of skills.

At this level, the nature of uncertainty seems to change from 'Can I do it?' - to a more complex level of wanting to deliver the very best experience possible, every time.

These teachers know they can do it; they've experienced classes that have gone exceptionally well, as well as those that, for whatever reason, were simply OK. They understand the very subtle differences between the two, and notice how a small comment, a smile or compliment at the right moment can swing the class from acceptable to brilliant.

They are not only experts in their subject, they are exceptional communicators with outstanding people skills and set the highest standards for themselves.

So, I can't promise you that with time and practice those nerves will completely disappear. Everyone will feel nervous at some point, but what's significantly different is that the emotion these experts experience could better be described as 'confident uncertainty'.

Meaning, I don't know what's going to happen but whatever it is, I'm confident I can deal with it.

So, don't be too hasty to conquer those nerves completely. Be quietly confident that whatever happens in the next few hours is fully under your control.

You are a Creative Professional - you CAN do it!

PERSONAL PRESENTATION

Self-confidence is all about how you feel in the classroom.

Of course, you want to feel calm, assured and in control of your students' progress as they learn. Feeling confident, gives you the freedom to relax and enjoy the experience of working with the wonderful creative projects you'll be sharing. You can be sure that if you can achieve that quiet, inner sense of 'confident uncertainty' that we talked about earlier, your students will also relax and feel secure in your ability to lead them through new and exciting techniques.

One of the most important qualities of a great teacher is being able to gain the confidence of your audience. We have already recognised the fact that for many adult learners the very idea of learning something new can be quite unnerving. Your pupils may feel nervous not only about entering a classroom for the first time in years but also about meeting you – the expert!

So, anything you can do to put your learners at ease, whilst at the same time, creating an air of confident professionalism, will be invaluable in helping to you deliver an ace classroom experience.

This is where personal presentation comes in. It's how you choose to present yourself to the outside world and especially, your customers. You may be the type of person who spends a long time choosing just the right outfit or puts considerable thought into what colours or hairstyle you wear. Then again, you might be more the wake-up and go type who is happy to let the world greet you as it finds you.

The image we present to our friends and colleagues is a unique part of our personal identity and something we are all aware of, even if it is sub-consciously.

Once you start teaching what you do, the image you present to your class and customers becomes more important. It's worth spending a few minutes to think about how you appear to others and why this is important.

HEALTH, SAFETY AND HYGIENE

If your creative skill is in any way linked to the production of food or cosmetics, for example, it will be imperative that you wear suitable clothing. Gloves, aprons, hairnets will be essential for you and your students. Be a shining example of everything you teach, if you request that your learners wear specific footwear in the workshop, make sure you do to. Cover any relevant aspects of personal protective wear at the start of the class and explain why it is important.

If your class routinely requires specific attire such as aprons, could this be an opportunity to show off your logo or personal branding? I've seen classes where all the students were provided with aprons advertising the teachers name and logo. A clever marketing trick which brings a professional, cohesive look to the class and encourages team bonding amongst the participants.

I've even seen branded items such as these aprons or notebooks or kit-bags being takeaways for the students to use at home afterwards. Clearly, this would need to be costed into the price of the class but what a great way to spread the word and ensure your customers continue to think of you long after they've left the classroom.

Exercise

Thinking about your own classes, are there any items you could use, wear or give away to students, showcasing your brand name of logo? Have a search online for the many companies who offer such products. Make a note of any that might be useful to you either now or in the future.

BRAND 'YOU'

Even if you decide not to go for something as obvious as logo'd attire, what you wear in class will still be a reflection of you and your personal 'brand'.

The clothes and colours you choose to wear, how you style your hair or nails will be the very first impression your customers have of you when they enter the classroom.

It would seem to me that there are very few creative spheres where dressing very formally is still de riguer. The very word 'creative' conjures up something less conventional and more imaginative but there is such diversity amongst our creative subjects that to draw any rules or suggest any universal guidelines would be impossible.

I hope it goes without saying that clean hair, nails – as far as possible – and clothes, will give a good impression. There is a subtle degree of respect inferred by being well presented. It may seem a rather old fashioned notion but your students are your customers who have paid to spend time with you.

If you take time to be suitably turned out, it implies that you appreciate their custom. Dressing for your craft is the key. Easy clothing that is representative of your style and subject will do the trick.

If your subject is jewellery, sewing, crochet or flower crowns – do wear your work. There is no better way to showcase your skill than by wearing it yourself. You are the greatest advocate for your subject and students love to see how their makes will look when worn. If you wear your work, there's a good chance they will too – more advertising for you. Great!

CONFIDENCE

Lastly, it will almost certainly give you confidence, knowing that you look good and feel good in what you've chosen to wear. Over time, you will probably develop a 'uniform' that works for you. When I teach, I'm often driving, lifting boxes, shifting chairs and tables as well as operating the kiln and talking to students. I like smartish jeans and easy tops with lots of pockets…!

Nobody wants to deal with a 'wardrobe malfunction' whilst they are teaching so keep it simple and suitable and definitely save your best shoes for another day – unless making shoes is your thing, of course, in which case wear them with pride…!

ACTION POINTS FROM THIS CHAPTER

- Create a checklist for each class to ensure every aspect has been thoroughly prepared.
- Practice positive thinking. Create a mental picture of you being a great teacher with lots of happy students.
- Think about how your work clothes and equipment can promote your personal brand
- If you make wearable art – wear it!
- Start to develop a teaching 'uniform' that is practical, presentable and reflects your personality and is suitable for your subject.

CHAPTER SIX

The Classroom

'Success is a science - if you have the conditions, you get the result'

Oscar Wilde

CREATING A LEARNING SPACE THAT WORKS FOR YOU AND YOUR STUDENTS

Key learning points in this chapter

- Your key considerations when setting up your classroom
- The importance of remembering names
- The benefits of providing all classroom equipment yourself
- Health & Safety essentials
- Classroom Etiquette; why you may need some additional rules.

The rise of the learning for leisure movement has generated a new type of classroom – almost every type of social space is being transformed into a place where people can gather to learn. Pubs, coffee bars, offices and shops can all make great creative spaces. Wherever you teach, there a few key rules to ensure everyone leaves safe and happy. This is what we're going to look at in this chapter.

For me, as a creative teacher, my greatest joy is NOT seeing my students go home with their beautiful silver jewellery – although this does always make me feel very proud. No, for me, the best part is when mid-lesson, I look around the classroom and see everyone chatting enthusiastically to each other and completely enjoying their experience. I love watching them share ideas and inspiration, admiring each other's work and planning their next creative adventure.

We've already discovered that making friends and social interaction are key motivators when choosing to attend a creative class. I know, for myself, that just spending time with likeminded folk can be both relaxing and inspiring. I've made some great friends in class and love find out more about everyone's artistic backgrounds – or lack of! Whether they be a Bluebell girl or a cabinet minister (yes, I've met both), it's always so interesting and informative to discover what brings people to a class.

Some time ago, I noticed and became interested in, how some groups just seem to hit it off and work together in a really creative way and others - well, don't. It would be easy to attribute this to the mix of individual personalities but I'm beginning to think there's more to it than this. In fact, I now believe that how I arrange the classroom or working space can have a significant effect on how students interact with each other.

So, wherever you find yourself running your classes it is so worthwhile putting some conscious thought into how you arrange the learning space.

Let's start with the basics. The essentials that will be common to most workspaces. Some creative fields such as cookery or printing will require more a specialist set-up but for most subjects, these are the key classroom ingredients you will need to consider.

SPACE

- Is the space available suitable for the number of students or does it limit numbers?
- How much space is needed per workstation allowing room to move and to accommodate any necessary equipment?

TABLES & CHAIRS

- Are tables or workbenches the correct height and will chairs be comfortable if sitting for most of the class? Always check what's provided in advance.

EQUIPMENT

- Can larger pieces of equipment be accommodated?
- Will students share tools or undertake certain tasks an allocated area?

DEMONSTRATIONS

- How & where will you position yourself for practical demonstrations?
- Will students gather round a central point or stay in their seats?
- How will you ensure everyone can see your demos clearly?
- Is there any technology available e.g. a docu-cam?

POWER SUPPLIES

- Check number and positioning of power points

FACILITIES

- Kitchen – for refreshments?
- Water supply – if needed for art/craft activities or cleaning up afterwards
- Toilets – essential!

'One of the challenges of teaching cross-stitch in winter, with evening classes or at some of those groovy, city venues can be the lack of good, natural light. I make sure I have lots of bright colours to work with…!' Mr X Stitch, Jamie Chalmers

There will always be a number of ways you can arrange the available space to accommodate students and it's how you do this that can either encourage interaction and conversation or stifle it.

Rather than have stand-alone work stations, I much prefer to push tables together and get students working in groups. I provide tools to share, which gets them talking and plan tasks that need to be completed in pairs which encourages conversation and team work.

Clearly, exactly how you do this will be determined by your subject and lesson plan but I find it immensely satisfying to see that my students have not only learned new practical and creative skills but had, fun, made friends and thoroughly enjoyed their class.

It's definitely worth putting that extra bit of thought into making the space really work for you.

EXERCISE

Make a plan of your ideal classroom set-up. Include individual workspaces, areas for specific tasks and the best position for demonstrations and explanations. Keep this as your blueprint and it will be easy to adapt to new venues.

Remembering Names – can you do it?

An important element in making learners feel welcome is to remember their names. Even if you think you have a terrible memory, it's worth making the effort as it really does make each person feel special if you address them by name.

Students often comment upon how quickly it I have learned and remembered their names – so how do I do it? Firstly, I'd like to say I don't have a great memory for names and I meet hundreds of students every year. I make a special effort to remember because I know how important it is in giving a positive impression of me, and my class.

Very often you will have booked students into your class, sold them tickets or answered pre-class queries. This should be a start in helping you to become familiar with who's who. On the day, I run through the list of attendees and try to commit the names to memory. Then, as soon as I meet the person, I try to say their name as many times as possible – hopefully without sounding too weird!

So, the conversation might go something like this

'Lovely to meet you, Linda'

'Linda, can I take your coat'

'And when you're ready, Linda, do help yourself to coffee in the kitchen'.

Something like that; you get the idea!

It also helps if students know each other's names, which brings us to the sticky problem of name labels. Personally, I'm not a fan of the 'on-your-chest' stick-on label, which curls up and falls off half way through the class.

I also hate staring at people's chests when I talk to them. Although, I must say I know lots of teachers who use these most effectively. Cardboard, pin-type badges or lanyards seem more professional and some can even be re-used.

Folded, tent-style name cards, which sit in front of each person's workplace can be helpful as long as you're not expecting students to move seats. For my own classes, I ask student to write their names onto their work mats so I can see it as I look over their shoulder. It works for me. I also ask students to say 'Hi' and introduce themselves to their neighbours at the start of each class, which helps to break the ice.

However you approach this, names are important and don't forget to make sure everyone knows your name, too!

'I believe the teacher is responsible for the atmosphere in the classroom. The students need to have complete confidence in you and feel they are in safe hands'. May Martin, Judge, Great British Sewing Bee.

TOOLS AND EQUIPMENT

Unless your class is completely fact based, it is inevitable that the use of tools, equipment and materials will be a big part of any practical learning experience.

Some of these will be absolute essentials, a camera for a photography class, for example. Others may be vital only for a small part of the process and some may be disposables, used for one class only.

It's worth considering, at the beginning, how students will purchase or access the tools, equipment and materials they are going to need.

'I try to keep a very co-ordinated, coherent, professional appearance with everything I use in my classes. It doesn't cost any more to be colour co-ordinated, so aprons, crockery and paperwork are always in my colours and printed with my logo'. Louise Talbot, Cutting the Curd, Cheese making Classes

There are different ways you might like to approach this;

Everything needed is provided by you

- You have complete control to ensure everyone has exactly the right amount of the right kit
- Can be expensive and replacements will be regularly needed.
- You might be able to sell specialist items or materials to students to supplement your income.
- Everyone is busy so students often appreciate not having to hunt around for specific items in the week prior to the class.

Students are issued with a list of essentials to buy beforehand

- If you issue a list of tools or materials to bring, ensure each item is used in class as people tend to resent spending out for kit that isn't used.

- It can be problematic if you are anticipating that students will arrive with the correct supplies but they turn up with something different / not suitable.
- Consider what might happen if the class is cancelled?

Inevitably, it is most likely that you will, as part of your start-up, need to invest in at least basic tools and equipment for your minimum number of students. Buy the best quality tools you can afford. They will get plenty of use and working with quality equipment will make yours and your students' lives easier and more pleasant. They will also need replacing less often and be less likely to let you down during a class.

'One of my biggest challenges was working out what tools and equipment I needed and budgeting for the expense of ten sets of kit for the first class. How much you need to spend can come as a surprise, but I broke it down and looked at what I needed immediately for the first class and bought that. Since then I've added to my stock as I've gone along'. Sian Hamilton, Editor, Making Jewellery Magazine

EXERCISE:

Start a shopping list of essential tools or equipment you'll need for your classes. Then do some online research to find the most cost effective suppliers.

HEALTH AND SAFETY

Other than subjects that involving knives, needles or other sharp objects, we don't tend to think of our creative work as being potentially dangerous. However, if used incorrectly, even everyday objects such as scissors can be harmful and it is your responsibility to be aware of and prepared for the full range of potential risks associated with your class. So, what do you need to consider?

- The Venue – make sure you know where fire exits are located as well as general fire drill procedures. It's important to familiarise students with these so they know what to do should an emergency occur.

- Tools, Equipment and Materials – even everyday objects or substances can present a health risk if used incorrectly. Make sure students understand how to use all tools and materials in the safest way. Ensure any portable electrical appliances have been PAT tested in line with regulations.

- First Aid – whilst I've never needed to administer anything more serious than a sticking plaster, undertaking a First Aid Certificate might help you to feel more confident should a minor emergency occur?

- COSHH Report - A venue may ask for a copy of your COSHH (Control of Substances Hazardous to Health) assessment. This will show you've considered the risks and have taken steps to reduce them. As a responsible tutor, it's worth spending time preparing this report. You'll find a lot of help online and once done will only need updating annually.

- Food Hygiene – If you serve food to your students or are preparing or making food in your class it will be inspected to make sure you are complying with food regulations. You may want to consider a Food Hygiene Certificate.

No one is expecting you to suddenly become a health & safety expert but most venues and class organisers will want you to have considered and prepared for any relevant health and safety issues. Acting now could save you time and potentially a great deal of money, later on.

'Many years ago a student had an epileptic fit in my class. Luckily, I knew how to deal with it and acted accordingly. The rest of the class were shaken but impressed that I dealt with it calmly. The teaching centre had not made me aware of the student's medical history. It's essential such important information is passed on to the tutor, they were lucky I knew what to do'. May Martin, Judge, The Great British Sewing Bee.

CLASSROOM ETIQUETTE

Whilst we're thinking about classroom etiquette, it's worth considering whether it may be necessary to set any further rules around how students behave in class.

- Smoking / Vaping – most venues are legally obliged to prevent customers from smoking or vaping on the premises but if your course involves a photo-walk, for example, you may want to extend this rule or you may be happy for students to smoke outside?

- Eating – will you allow students to eat or snack at their desks or set aside a specific area for eating? A lot of venues ban hot drinks at work stations because of the damage a spilt drink can cause.

- Photos — A tricky one. If a student asks to photograph your work it can be flattering, but you might like to set some parameters around how and where such photos can be used.

- If you plan to take photos of students working in class it's wise to ask for permission to do so. If you teach children, you will need written consent from their parents or carers.

- Videos — I've experienced a couple of incidences where students have openly set up a recording device and filmed my demos or presentations. The first time this happened, I was rather taken aback and probably didn't respond, as I should have done. In fact I didn't say anything. In an age where intellectual property and information are your greatest assets it may avoid an awkward situation if you have a clearly stated policy around video in class.

ACTION POINTS FROM THIS CHAPTER

- Thinking about the structure of your class. Are there any ways you can encourage conversation and teamwork?
- Make a classroom checklist for new venues so you know everything you need will be available.
- Photograph your classroom set up at the start of the day and add notes on how well it worked so you can repeat or adjust for future classes.
- List essential equipment you'll need to purchase. If students are to provide their own materials, draft a list.
- Carefully consider any Health & Safety requirements related to classroom activities.

CHAPTER SEVEN

Pricing and Payment Methods

'Price is what you pay –
Value is what you get'

Warren Buffet

TIPS AND ADVICE TO HELP YOU SUCCESSFULLY PRICE YOUR CLASSES

Key learning points in the chapter

- Why being nice doesn't pay!
- The essential market research you need to be doing - now.
- Calculating the true cost of your classes
- Why becoming an 'Expert' is your key to earning more.
- Why you need a cancellation and refunds policy

When starting to plan your very first class there's a lot to think about; not only when and where you will teach but should you have a website and how will you promote yourself on social media? I'm guessing that somewhere near the very top of this list of mental conundrums will be; how much should I charge for my classes...?

This is a tricky subject to deal with because I know that, as creatives, we all want to be nice.

We tend not to be natural business people and thinking about money makes us feel a bit, well, uncomfortable. We want people to like us. We want people to admire our work and hopefully, even buy it. And most of all we want people to sign up for our wonderful workshops. I sense that at the back of your mind is the thought, well, 'it doesn't matter if I don't much money' - from my first few classes, 'I'll be happy if people just show up and enjoy themselves and it's all good experience for me'. Am I right...?

OK, so let's think this through. What's likely to happen if we adopt this approach...?

In Chapter One we looked at where you might be now in your career and how teaching what you do might fit into your working life. If you are unable to turn a viable profit from your classes, the cash to continue will have to come from elsewhere. You might be ok with using funds from your day job or your savings to subsidise this new venture but in the long term, this is not sustainable, and you'll end up poorer than when you started.

Much better, to be realistic as to what your outgoings are and therefore what you need to earn. By adopting this approach from the outset you will be building a sustainable small business that will bring pleasure to your life and to the lives of countless others for many years to come.

So, onwards.

The question I get asked most often is how will I know how much to charge for my classes? I wish there was a quick, straight-forward response to this. Life would be so much easier if there was a set answer or an easy formula I could share with you to solve this problem.

However, what I do know is that there are a number of key considerations and an equal number of lesser variables to bring into the picture when creating the perfectly priced class.

MARKET RESEARCH

Let's begin with some good news - you've probably already started your market research without even realising it. Most likely you will have attended some creative classes yourself in the recent past, so you'll know how much you paid and what you personally feel is an acceptable price to learn new skills. So, let's take this to the next stage and actively research the learning market.

To get us started there are three factors you'll find it helpful to look at

- Subject Specific
- Geographical
- Level of expertise

Research: Subject Specific

Start by researching classes in your subject .This will give a good comparison as to what other teachers, like you, are charging. Delve into the class descriptions, learning outcomes, resources provided and the venue. You'll quickly begin to appreciate how difficult it can be to compare one class to another.

Can you compare a half-day class to a full day in the same subject? One venue may include lunch or a glass of Prosecco, others advise students to bring sandwiches. I've worked with venues that provide nothing, not even a hot drink. This seems a little mean. Maybe they weren't fully on top of 'the customer experience' but clearly, every little extra must be costed in.

So, although the subject may be the same, comparing one class to another may not immediately give us a clear idea of the 'going-rate'.

Comparing the class content, objectives or learning outcomes might be more efficient. But not all class programmes gives you that information.

Research: Geographical

If you know where you will be teaching, it can be helpful to look around at the cost of classes locally. You may start to notice an average price for evening courses, day classes or weekend workshops. Without doubt, all classes and events held in bigger cities will attract a premium. The higher costs of venues, travel etc., all add to an overall higher price. A greater pool of potential students can also push prices up. If you can find similar classes in your area great, otherwise your findings here will just be something to add into the overall equation.

Research: Level of Expertise

By now, I hope you're getting a feel for how classes are generally priced in your subject and in your local area. The next factor to consider is the perceived level of experience and expertise of the teacher.

Teaching advanced techniques in any field attracts premium. These skills take years to master not to mention countless hours of practice, failed attempts and wasted materials whilst the master refines his or her trade. Across the country there may only be one or two teachers who will reach these giddy heights of expertise and they will attract a devoted following of keen fans eager to attend their classes.

You'll notice I said 'perceived' level of expertise because we also have a new breed of celebrity teachers who have found fame in a different genre.TV presenters, for example, who support or champion a specific creative area and then combine careers to present classes. Whether they have an established creative skill set or not, the celebrity tag can undoubtedly command higher prices and attract a wider audience.

I'm guessing that if you're reading this book you are not a celebrity teacher – but maybe it's something to aim for!

EXERCISE

Create a table or spreadsheet to populate as you research your market. Look online or locally and keep note of any similarities or differences to your own classes. It will be very helpful to have all this information in one place and easier to notice trends and make comparisons at a glance.

CALCULATING COSTS

Until now, our market research has been general rather than specific but you should already be getting a feel for the range of prices currently out there. For our next exercise, we're going to think specifically about you and your class. Unless you want your teaching to become an unpaid hobby, you must ensure you are covering all your costs – at the very least. So what are those costs likely to be?

COST: Your Time

At the time of writing, the national living wage is around £8.00 per hour so make this your absolute minimum. However, as a skilled artisan you can almost certainly charge more than this. If you are a very highly experienced and respected creative professional, I recommend you charge a LOT more. We already know that customers appreciate learning from this calibre of teacher and will pay more for the pleasure of meeting you and learning with you.

It's important also to decide if you will charge only for the hours you spend in front of the class, actually teaching or will you include preparation, planning and possibly travel time, too? I know teachers who do both so there's no right or wrong here but clearly the difference can be considerable.

COST: Your Expertise

Do not underestimate your expertise; it is your most valuable commodity. Your customers are paying to learn from you; they are buying in to your knowledge. Your students benefit from the time you've spent honing your craft, the techniques you have practised over time and the mistakes you made. Even the classes and courses that you've paid for to reach a level where you are now competent to teach what you do. Please don't undersell yourself and your incredible creative talent.

COST: Venue

Whether it is a room in a pub, a village hall or a beautiful boutique hotel, if you've procured the venue for your event, there will be a cost to take into account. It's always wise to visit the venue in advance, chat with the owner or manager and make sure you fully understand what you are paying for. You should also check the price quoted includes

- Heating / lighting
- Provision of tables / chairs
- Any catering arrangements
- Access for setting up in advance
- Inclusion in any marketing or promotional material produced by the venue

Venues such as village halls are often bookable by the hour. Rather than book just the advertised hours of the class, make sure you include at least an hour for setting up at the start of the day and probably the same for packing and tidying up at the end.

I remember one particularly busy workshop day when I'd planned to finish at 4.00pm only to find the hall was booked for a children's party starting at 4.00pm. I am now very careful to make sure I have packing up time even if it means paying for an extra hour. It's worth it to finish the day in peace and quiet....!

Even if you are teaching at home, although the venue may appear to be 'free' don't forget there are still costs involved

- Heating / lighting
- Wear & tear
- Provision of refreshments or lunch
- Relevant insurances needed

COST: Materials

If your class is going to involve the use of any kind of materials whether it is paint, fabric, flowers, flour or a precious metal, if you have undertaken to provide those materials yourself, their cost must be included in the price of the class.

I feel, at this point, it will be worthwhile to make a slight detour away from pricing to consider the pros and cons of providing class materials yourself, as there is a direct link to costs

Pros –the good points of providing class materials

- Peace of mind from knowing all students will have the correct materials
- Saves time in class – any preparation can be done in advance
- If you can source at cost price you may be able to make a small profit
- You may also be able to sell additional materials during / after the class
- Students often appreciate everything for the class being provided on the day so all they need to do is turn up.

Cons – the downside

- Sourcing and ordering supplies can be time consuming
- Are you able to store goods in the correct conditions until they are needed?
- The advance expense is entirely yours

And then compare these to the scenario of students bringing materials with them.

Pros – of students bringing their own materials

- Saves the time you might have spent sourcing materials in advance of the class
- No upfront costs for you

Cons – the downside of the above

- You will need to ensure students receive a list of materials to bring with them, well in advance of the class
- Risk of students not sourcing the correct materials – or forgetting completely!
- May take time at the start of the class to check suitability
- Students can begrudge spending on any materials that are not used in class, for whatever reason.

So, clearly there are two schools of thought here. Is it best to provide class resources yourself or expect students to bring supplies with them? I know teachers who work successfully in both ways. One may immediately stand out as being the better option for you, or you may wish to try both and then decide.

My own preference is to provide everything needed for the class, myself. I value the peace of mind from knowing that everyone will have exactly the right amount of the correct supplies for each project. And, because students who have enjoyed their class often want to take supplies home having the option to sell extra materials can provide a small but useful additional income.

'Working with natural ingredients that can vary in quality can create challenges. I provide everything needed at my classes and try to use milk and ingredients from local producers as it creates a wonderful end product'. Louise Talbot, Cutting the Curd Cheese making Classes

COST: Use of tools and equipment

When we think about the materials used in class we're thinking about items such as yarn or foliage that will be used up in the creative process. These could also be called consumables, as they will – in most cases – only be used once.

Most creative classes also involve the use of some specialist tools or equipment. These are different from materials in that they can be re-used for many classes only needing to be replaced at regular intervals.

As the expert in your subject, I would generally advise that it is best for you to provide the essential tools and equipment for your students. You will have a good grasp of the range of equipment available and what will be both suitable and durable for the class. Choose the best quality you can afford.
It will undoubtedly cost more initially but it will make life easier for your students to work with good quality tools, give better results and last longer. However, quality equipment can be expensive and needs to be maintained and replaced regularly. Make sure you build these ongoing costs into the price of your classes, from the start.

It's not too difficult, once you're fully kitted out, to divide the total cost over the length of time or number of workshops you expect the equipment to be used.

COST: Website / marketing

In Chapter Eight we look at cost effective ways of promoting your classes, including whether you might need to invest in a website. Whatever you decide, the cost of building, maintaining, updating and eventually replacing the site, as well as any other expenditure on advertising, social media promotions or printing, needs to be added into your costs.

COST: Travel / Meals / Accommodation

Once you become accustomed to your new role of being a teacher, you may start to look further afield for work. This could involve either using your own car or public transport as well as potentially spending nights away from home and the need to feed yourself.

Personally, I love being on the go and am delighted that my teaching has given me the opportunity to travel, both around the UK and further afield. I've been to places I know I would never otherwise have visited and met many wonderful people. However, as lovely as is to travel, it can be expensive. I always include travel costs and accommodation in quotes to new venues, who in turn, add this into the price they charge students for the class.

I worked a few years ago with a beautiful venue in a very picturesque part of the country who made a policy of not paying tutors any accommodation, subsistence or travel expenses.

I loved teaching there and everyone was so friendly but eventually I did the maths and worked out that the total expense for the trip was almost directly equivalent to the amount I got paid. So, although I enjoyed it, it was a lot of work for very little financial gain. So, very reluctantly I decided that it didn't make business sense to continue with this venue.

These are the sort of decisions you will need to make for your business but you can only decide once you've done the maths and are fully informed to the true cost of each event.

EXERCISE

Create a table or spreadsheet to help you calculate your costs. Populate the rows with estimates initially and adjust to the actual prices as you make purchases. Keep this information up to date as prices change and you'll always have an accurate, current record of your class costs. Start a list of items to include here:

'One of my biggest challenges has been in creating an economically viable business model. Initially, I was still working in my day job so could keep my costs low. I still aim to keep my workshop prices 'all inclusive' with no hidden extras and I always give students lots of free stuff, too. I get great pleasure from giving things away - I believe its good karma...!' Jamie Chalmer, Mr X Stitch

OTHER VARIABLES TO CONSIDER

So, we've looked at the measurable factors that contribute to your class running costs – time, venue, materials etc. In addition to these are a plethora of less tangible issues that can still influence your final price.

Technical Complexity

I am encouraging you to plan your first classes around a project or creative skill that can be easily managed by either complete beginners or those with a basic knowledge of your subject. This will be easiest to start with but once you feel confident and have more classroom experience you may want to teach more technically challenging topics.

Upgrading your teaching makes life more interesting and challenging for you and is a great way to promote your expertise. Even better, you can almost certainly charge more for teaching more advanced skills.

Kudos

We've already mentioned the rise of the 'celebrity' teacher but you don't need to be a celebrity to have a faithful following of students. Social media has created new opportunities for us to tell our story and engage a worldwide audience. Instagram 'Influencers' are using the power of social media to promote themselves, their products and those of other like-minded businesses. Their voice is powerful and followers are keen to know their thoughts – some are almost becoming celebrities in their own right.

Join them and you too could be seen as having greater value as a teacher – strange but true.

Seeing your name in print can be very exciting as well as giving your personal brand a massive lift. If you've written articles, contributed to national or professional press or best of all, written a book, you are well on the way to becoming a recognised 'expert' and your ideas, techniques and teaching of greater value.

Location

I mentioned earlier that in general, the cost of classes in our major cities is likely to be higher than elsewhere. This is a direct reflection of the higher costs of travel, premises and many other contributing factors. These costs will already have been taken into account, earlier in this chapter.

However, in addition to this, a very prestigious or aspirational venue will, quite possibly although not always, cost you more. However the potential for charging more is also increased. As a teacher, I love to work in beautiful surroundings and am lucky to be invited to teach in some wonderful venues. For students, who often see a creative class as a special treat, a boutique or beautiful venue adds an intangible sense of value to the day, which can then be reflected in your prices.

Number of students

The number of students you are prepared to teach in a group or who can be comfortably accommodated in the space available will influence the amount you can charge per person.

For fixed costs such as the price of the venue, heating and lighting, when divided amongst fewer people equates to a higher cost per person. This is fairly straightforward but also consider that smaller groups will enable you to spend more time with each participant and this can be of great value.

Students are paying for your time and your knowledge so the more they have, the more they may be willing to spend.

Another scenario could be the possibility of teaching 1:1 lessons. This might be something you could offer as a personalised day as it lends itself to more challenging and technical knowledge. A bespoke session could be made by special arrangement with a student who prefers to have your full attention. Either way, a single student should expect to pay maybe two or three times the 'per person' rate of joining a larger group.

Your Customer Base

Once you've taken all of the above into account and know that you have covered all your costs and are making a profit, the spending power of your customer base may be yet another factor to consider when setting your prices. If your subject lends itself towards university students, young parents or those of retirement age you may need be conscious of keeping the cost affordable.

Rather than cut your profit, try to look at areas where costs could be lower – a more cost-effective venue, for example, or less expensive materials. Personally, I love the opportunity to share my passion for making jewellery with groups who may not consider this something they could afford to do.

Teaching is a gift and being creative makes people happy. If I can spread a little happiness, then I'm honoured and privileged to do so.

Popularity of your Classes

I remember in the early days I was happy if two or three people booked for my class. The thought of being able to fill every place was still a dream. But, gradually my dream came true and now most of my classes fill up quite easily and many have a waiting list. But this took time. Over the years, I've been able to tweak class content, ditch the venues that weren't working for me until slowly a successful formula started to become visible and those classes really took off.

So, once you have a popular class that is (almost) guaranteed to fully book, why not experiment with raising the price just a little. Interestingly, in most cases, I've found this doesn't affect the bookings at all.

In conclusion….

I am very conscious that I've written reams on the subject of pricing your classes. As mentioned at the very beginning, I wish there was a simple formula I could share that would give the perfect price every time but I'm sorry there isn't.

Every one of the above factors will, to differing extents, add to the equation giving you a sensible final figure. Read them through, decide how they apply to your situation or subject and give it your very best guess. My feeling is, you'll get it pretty much spot on.

The most important message here is – do not undersell your knowledge and creative talents.

WHEN THE VENUE SETS THE PRICE

All of the above applies only to situations where you are planning, promoting and organising classes in your own name. This is a lot of work and a lot of responsibility for which you need to be fairly remunerated by setting your prices correctly. However, there is a notable exception to this situation, where you have been invited to teach at a college or similar venue that has their own, set rate of pay for tutors.

To be completely clear, this means that none of the above variables apply. You will be paid the same amount whatever the technical complexity of your class, or however famous you are!

About half of all the venues I teach at fall into this category and in some ways it makes life a lot easier.

The venue or college take responsibility for advertising your course, taking bookings, answering student queries and processing payments. In return, they will have a common rate of pay for all teachers. This can save you a lot of time and importantly, when the venue promotes your course to their own audience, your message will be reaching a large number of potential students who are completely new to you.

This single fact can make it really worthwhile to cultivate a reliable round of well-respected venues to promote your classes. Over the years, I've met many students who have become loyal followers and subsequently attended my own classes, via another teaching venue.

Once you have made contact with the venue – see Chapter Eight for more information on finding and approaching venues – and know their daily / hourly rate for tutors, check carefully if it includes

- Planning & preparation time
- Travel expenses
- Accommodation
- Meals or a subsistence allowance

You may also want to ask

- The number of students you will be expected to teach
- If the venue expects commission from any sales you make during the class.

With this information you should be able to make an informed decision as to whether this will be a financially viable offer and respond accordingly.

HOW WILL STUDENTS PAY?

So far, in this chapter, we've spent a lot of energy analysing variables and calculating costs and prices. It's almost easy to forget that probably the most important part of the whole business is collecting payments.

In our most recent example, where the venue is doing most of the work and simply paying a daily rate, this is something we don't need to worry about.
All the work will be done by the venue. But if you are planning, promoting and hosting your own events this is a vital step.

VIA YOUR WEBSITE

If you have decided you need a website, you may be thinking of including a function whereby students can not only see your upcoming classes but also purchase a ticket direct. Therefore, you will need a 'Payment Gateway' so customers can pay online with a credit or debit card. Your web designer will be able to advise you of the best way to do this. Technology is changing rapidly and options are becoming more flexible, user friendly and cost effective.

Probably the most important consideration here is make it very, very easy for customers to pay. Of course, you want a system that will be simple for you to administer but in this age of impatience, the quicker and slicker you can make your payment process, the less likely you'll be to loose potential sales along the way.

The past two or three years have seen major advances in ticket sale technology and online payment systems.

VIA EVENT AND TICKETING WEBSITES

A Google search will throw up a growing number of bespoke websites who will list your event and sell tickets on your behalf. Most are easy to navigate and free to list your course.

In general, you pay a small commission when a ticket is sold but this does vary so read through the small print before deciding which is best for you. This can be a great way for students to find you and sign up for your brilliant classes.

Some you might like to investigate

- Craftcourses
- Eventbrite
- Billetto
- Ticket tailor
- Eventbee

VIA PAYPAL

PayPal is a universal success story that processes payments and is easily accessible for small businesses. It is free to create an account and PayPal take a small commission from each transaction.

VIA SOCIAL MEDIA

Business accounts with some social media platforms include the ability to sell products and offer discounts as well as set up events. Investigate your accounts, check costs and keep up to date with new offerings as they change rapidly.

TAKING FACE TO FACE OR TELEPHONE PAYMENTS

For a long time, I only took cash or cheque payments for my courses but as both seem quite quickly to have become almost obsolete a card payment method is now almost essential. Options include;

Card reader

A card reader is a handy little portable gadget that enables you to take online payments directly from a customer. You've probably experienced this if you've ever bought from a small business at a craft fair or a market.

The beauty of taking credit and debit cards is that you don't need to carry vast amounts of cash or change and payments are automatically credited into your bank account. Set-up costs and commission charges vary. Some you might like to investigate

- Izettle
- PayPal – have their own card reader
- Square
- Sum Up

PDQ Machine

PDQ stands for Process Data Quickly but these are more commonly known as a Credit Card machine – the type you would use in a shop. There are many payment companies providing this service but until your transactions exceed £1000 per month a simple card reader (see above) is probably best for you.

It's worth re-iterating that a simple and seamless system for taking payments will benefit your business from day one. So spend some time thinking about how, where and when your customers will pay and make it as easy as possible for them and for yourself.

Cancellation Policy & Refunds

Whist you are calculating the perfect price for your class. You may also like to be considering if you will have a cancellation policy or offer refunds?

A cancellation policy is likely to apply if a student is unable to attend the class, once they have paid. As soon as you start planning your class, costs begin to be incurred. You may need to pay for the venue, buy materials or order refreshments. Some of these may not be refundable if the class doesn't run.

Very occasionally, you may need to cancel a class yourself. This could be because of

- Insufficient number of bookings to make the class viable.
- Problems with the venue
- Extreme weather conditions
- Personal reasons or other unforeseen circumstances

Therefore, having a clear policy about how much you will or will not refund and under what circumstances or timescales will prevent you from being out of pocket should the worst happen. It will also avoid awkward conversations with customers who may assume they will be entitled to a full refund.

Ensuring that your policy is added to your website and booking forms will make it easier to deal effectively with any future requests for refunds.

'Cancelling workshops due to last winter's severe weather has been one of our most challenging situations and created some uncomfortable discussions. It's vital to have a fair policy in place to help sort things out to everyone's satisfaction'. Simon Sonsino, Director Ardington school of Crafts

ACTION POINTS FROM THIS CHAPTER

- Begin your market research. Record any useful findings, as these will help you build an accurate picture of current prices.
- Start calculating the potential cost of providing the necessary tools and equipment. Will students bring their own materials or will you provide these too?
- Investigate options for taking payments.
- Consider how you can best process card payments.
- Draft a cancellation policy.

CHAPTER EIGHT

Promoting Your Classes

'Without promotion -
something terrible happens ... nothing!'

P.T Barnum

IT'S TIME TO TELL THE WORLD ABOUT YOUR WONDERFUL CLASSES.

Key learning points in this chapter

- Why existing customers are your best asset
- How to create a simple email newsletter
- Deciding if you need a website
- Making the most of social media without it taking over your life
- The benefits of an events listing website
- The pros and cons of magazine advertising

I'm so pleased we've got this far. I hope by now you have a great lesson plan and some sound ideas on when and where you will be teaching your first class. I'm sure you don't need me to tell you that however brilliant this amazing new venture may be, it won't be a sell-out success unless your customers know about it.

Self-promotion doesn't always come easily to us creative types. We tend to prefer to just get on with doing what we do and trust in the brilliance of our work to get us noticed. You might be thinking the same about your classes.

Not so much 'Why will they come? ' as 'Why wouldn't they ...?'

We already know that attending a class, learning and being creative are the new social events in our calendars. It's great to have something in the diary to look forward to but everyone is sooooooo busy nowadays that in this noisy, fast moving world it can be really difficult to gain customers attention let alone the commitment to sign up for a class.

There's an old adage from the world of marketing, which says that a new customer needs to see or hear about your product or service seven times before they consider buying from you. It's worth keeping this in mind. It reinforces the fact that filling a class will take some considerable effort to bring it to the attention of potential students – it doesn't just happen.

Over time, as you become better known for your teaching and your classes gain in popularity, a natural momentum occurs which makes selling seats so much easier. Right now we need to start that ball rolling and the good news is there are some easy and very cost effective ways to do this.

Existing Customers

I believe in making the most of what you have – in life and in teaching. If you currently work in a creative field or make to sell, it's very likely you already have a set of existing loyal customers.

These people know you and (I'm guessing) already admire your work so are very likely to be interested in your new venture and positively receptive to new opportunities to engage with you.

A quick mention here about General Data Protection Rules; we all hate being inundated with spam sales emails and annoying newsletters. So the industry has, quite rightly, tightened up the rules for how we use, share and store personal information such as email addresses. Check you are GDPR compliant before sending any information to existing customers.

Sending an e-newsletter

I have a great deal of success with email newsletters because they arrive in the inbox of people who I know are interested in what I do and want to hear from me.

Sending a short, friendly e-newsletter to a few hundred people can be a simple and cost effective way to get your message out there. Even better, if you use one of the many free services available, such as MailChimp, creating professional looking, mobile-friendly content is quick, easy and free!

There are a number of online newsletter services you might like to investigate. The features they offer vary and are regularly updated so it's worth comparing a few to help you make the right choice.

Have a look at

- MailChimp
- Constant Contact
- Drip
- Aweber
- Get Response

Keep newsletters short and to the point – nobody wants to scroll down for hours, if at all – and include a photo image of what customers can expect to make at the class. Don't forget the important info; when, where, costs and a link to your website, if you have one. Plus clear instructions on how to buy a ticket or contact you for further information.

Here's an example of a really simple email newsletter

LOGO AND NAME

Exciting news about my new venture!

I want you to be first to hear about my new classes in Silver smithing. Come and spend a day with me learning the basics of contemporary jewellery making. Learn how to roll, texture, polish and finish a gorgeous silver ring, which will be ready to wear home. Suitable for beginners. Lots of fun and cake guaranteed!

Photo image

Date: Venue: Cost:

Book Now

Remember, the easier you can make it for a potential customer to book their seat the more likely they are to join up. So include as many direct links as possible to the booking page on your website or your ticket provider.

How else could you make the most of existing customers? A few ideas ....

- If you work in a gallery or sell your work, pop a leaflet in with purchases
- Invite them to a free or discounted class in return for a review
- Engage them in a poll on any aspect of your classes – people like to feel involved.
- Ask for suggestions on potential venues
- Add a LATEST NEWS line to your email signature

YOUR WEBSITE

Something else I've noticed about creatives, is that we have an above-average tendency to be technophobes. You know, that very worrying sense that the rest of the world understands exactly how a website works and whilst we know it could be important it's beyond us to fathom it out.

And yet, if we want to find out what time the library closes, how much a new tyre for the car will cost or if tickets are still available for that concert - what's the first thing we do? Go online and look for the website.

Recently, I've found myself pondering on the relevance of a website in today's world where social media is often the driving force behind news and events. I know some small businesses who have made a start without a website, relying on platforms such as Etsy, EBay and Facebook to be their voice in the world. However, my underlying thought is that having a simple website or at least a page where potential customers can go to find out more, makes good business sense.

The good news here, is that you are not alone - there are now online services such as SquareSpace or Shopify who provide very helpful templates and 24 hour assistance for the terrified. The very essence of these services is that they are there to make it easy for those with absolutely no technical knowledge whatsoever to create and maintain a beautiful website – that's what they're there for. So get to know them and find out what they can do for you. There's no reason to be embarrassed by a lack of knowledge – they will have heard it all before!

What if you don't have a big budget for marketing or a website? The real beauty of these sites is that most cost nothing to create but charge a monthly fee for their service or take a commission on sales. Provided you stick to the free templates etc there are no upfront costs. Perfect.

Before you start, my advice would be to do some research on how to best to present yourself online. Look at some of the big names in your industry or someone you admire. Check colours, fonts, images. Notice that often their websites are very simple. Simple is good for your customers and will be easy for you to update and maintain.

Checklist of what to include in your first website

- Logo and Business name
- A couple of sentences summing up what you are all about
- Great images
- Class dates, venues, prices
- Contact information
- Social media links

Images

Just a word here about the photo images you use for your site - they are very important. A good photo can be worth a thousand words in helping to sell classes.

You'll want to portray your events as fun, sociable, inspiring and maybe even aspirational? Sell the sense that this is going to be an enjoyable experience. Photos of the process and any final products can be hugely helpful in persuading potential students to sign up or find out more. My experience is that people like to have a clear idea of what they will learn or make before parting with their money.

Eventually, you may want to invest in some professional photos but in the meantime, learn how to use your camera or mobile phone to take great shots and get a few second opinions on which ones best represent your new venture.

SOCIAL MEDIA

The importance of social media in our lives has increased dramatically in the last five years and it's more than likely, that you will already have accounts with one or two of the main players.

You may even already be using social media to promote your creative career. So much has been and continues to be written about it that I don't intend to join the ranks of social media gurus', telling you how to promote your accounts and gain followers, here.

But, however you look at it, social media is big and can be an incredibly useful tool in getting your message out to the world. Even better, a large part of it can be completely free.

If you are new to social media, make a start with just one of the main platforms and get confident before moving into the others. My advice would be to just aim for 2 or 3 posts a week, definitely not more than one a day to keep things manageable. Feel free to browse around on other peoples accounts see what they're writing about and join in the online conversations. It's called 'social' for a reason.

If you are completely stuck on what to post about, here are a few ideas

- Share pictures of your students with their makes – great publicity!
- Behind the scenes pictures of you preparing for your class
- Photos of your everyday tools and equipment and why you love them
- Piles of fabric, yarn or whatever colourful materials you use can be very eye-catching
- Top tips are always appreciated...!
- Pose a question and invite discussion
- New classes or new dates
- What went wrong – use this carefully but it makes you look human which can be very appealing!

If you are new to, or nervous about using social media, it's a good idea to find a class or workshop that will help you get to grips with the basics, the best way to set up your account and how to use the many online tools and options available. If you're reading this book, it may be that you're planning to teach classes helping others to manage their social media or take lovely photos of their makes, in which case, you might be able to teach us all something!

Always remember that the likes of Facebook and Twitter are in fact, profit making organisations so will do everything they can to encourage you to pay extra for adverts and promotions. Some of these can still be incredibly good value when compared to more traditional advertising and may be worth considering but to start with there's a lot you can do for free.

Social media is also incredibly fast moving, in terms of updates, new features and the dreaded algorithms. It can almost be too fast and can easily get overwhelming but remember social media is your friend. It's also a brilliant way to stay in contact with past students by encouraging them to like or follow you. You can even create 'invitation only' groups, which can be like an online club for like-minded learners.

'If you have the means and the capacity, you owe it to yourself to exploit social media'. Jamie Chalmers, Mr X Stitch

EVENT LISTINGS WEBSITE

Event listings websites can help boost your online presence and have two main advantages

- By listing your event you add all the details of your class to the site so customers can read about it, see photographs and discover details such as times, price and venue all in one place.
- If someone likes the look of your class, they can book directly through the site.

Most are free to list but take a small commission from any ticket sales and then forward the profits of those sales directly to your bank account. The good news here is if you don't sell any tickets it doesn't cost you anything – but let's not be negative!

The features they offer and commission rates vary so make a comparison to choose the best one for you. Some you might like to look at

- www.eventbrite.co.uk
- www.billetto.co.uk
- www.chooseyourevent.co.uk
- www.Britevents.com
- www.wherecanwe
- go.com
- www.Evvnt.com

VENUE LED MARKETING

So far, we've looked at how to promote classes where you are personally responsible for all the admin arrangements – setting the dates, finding the venue and selling tickets.

But there is another possibility, which is when a venue or organisation has booked you to deliver your class at their school, club or premises.

In this situation you may have prospected the host as part of your marketing activities or they might have contacted you directly with an invitation to teach. I love it when this happens. It's always a great compliment to hear that a respected venue has heard of you and your work and wants to offer you a potential job.

It's also interesting to see how venues share information about good teachers and successful classes so it's worth making the effort to get your name known as hopefully more bookings will follow....!

However, the real beauty of being invited to teach at a creative venue is they will very actively be marketing your event to their own audience. They will be advertising locally, sending information to their newsletter groups, promoting to their fans and followers via social media and adding your details into any printed programmes or leaflets they produce. In short, this means a whole new audience of potential customers will hear about you. These are most probably people who aren't currently aware of you and whom it would be unlikely you could reach on your own.

Therefore, it's really important that any information or images you provide to the venue for their own marketing purposes are as good as you can possibly make them. In general a new venue will ask for the following information

- A short biography of you and your creative experience
- Photo image of yourself
- A short course description – around 50 words
- A longer course description – around 150 words
- Costing details including any payable by students on the day
- Promotional images such as examples of work students will produce in the class

Take time to find some appealing images and ensure your course descriptions are clear and concise. Remember that although they will appear under the name of the venue any information you supply will reflect your personal brand as well as helping to promote your classes. It also makes life a great deal easier for the venue admin staff if you can be prompt and efficient with your information. It's always good to build a reputation as being friendly and easy to work with – that way you'll be far more likely to be invited back!

So, the best venues will be working very hard to fill your classes and promoting you at the same time. But don't leave it all to them.

This is a two-way street and venues love it if you do your bit, too. So, post about how much you're looking forward to the day, how excited you are to be teaching at this wonderful new venue and don't forget to add their dates to your website.

Two more things it's wise to keep in mind when you're teaching on behalf of another organisation;

1. For the hours you're delivering your class, you become the face of that organisation to your students. It's important that everything you do reflects the values and principles of the establishment. Happy students will not only extol the virtues of your class but also recommend the venue to their friends.

2. The same is also true if any part of their experience is not up to scratch – it reflects badly on the venue as well as yourself.

Always make a point of writing – email is fine – to the organiser afterwards to thank them for the day and say how much you enjoyed being there. This is a great help in building a great long term working relationship and your reputation as being a pleasant and professional person to work with.

TRADITIONAL ADVERTSING

Magazines

Interestingly, when I run this subject as a face-to-face class and I ask new teachers how they are thinking of promoting their classes, traditional advertising routes such as magazines are usually first to be mentioned.

So let's look at the pros and cons of magazine advertising

PROS

- Reaches a targeted specialist interest audience
- Potential nationwide group of new customers
- Kudos by association with a respected 'glossy

CONS

- Can be very expensive
- Difficult to accurately measure cost effectiveness
- Short shelf- life?

Personally, I've never found the paid advertising route in magazines to be terribly effective, for the above reasons. It is possible to evaluate the potential reach of an ad via readership numbers and distribution but you need to be quite marketing savvy to make sense of the numbers.

Big companies obviously do this and find it worthwhile but they have vast advertising budgets and I'm guessing that at this point you don't. My advice would be to look at some of the more cost effective methods of getting your message heard before parting with your hard earned cash.

However, if seeing your name in a glossy still appeals a couple of points to try

- Investigate any no or low cost opportunities – offer a free place for a reporter in return for a class review, for example.
- 'Advertorials' appear in the main body of the magazine rather than the adverts section.
- Test the water by contacting a couple of existing advertisers in a chosen publication and ask if they've found it to be beneficial.

LEAFLETS & FLYERS

You may already have a business card for your creative day job that will double up when you start promoting your classes. Even in today's digital world new contacts will still often ask for a business card so having your name and contact details ready to share is almost an essential.

In addition, there are some really beautiful contemporary business card designs available that can carry an image of your work and so double as an advertisement, too.

So apart from a business card, what other printed promotional material might be useful? In some situations a simple leaflet or flyer might be a good option.

For example, if you get the opportunity to show your work at a gallery or open evening, a flyer could help to introduce customers to your classes. Sometimes event organisers create a 'goody bag' for attendees and might be willing to include your leaflet.

Leaflets are not an essential in your promotional strategy but they can play a part. The good thing is they are not expensive and a local printer could probably create several hundred for you for less than £50.00.

ACTION POINTS FROM THIS CHAPTER

- Think about how you can tell your existing customers about your classes.
- Investigate email newsletter providers and set up a free account.
- Look at self-build website platforms and identify one that might be suitable for you.
- If you are not comfortable with social media, sign up for a class to learn the basics.
- Browse over some of the suggested events listing sites and think about how they might work for you.

CHAPTER NINE

Trouble Shooting

'It isn't what we say or think that defines us – but what we do'

Jane Austin

THE WAY YOU REACT TO A SITUATION CAN MAKE ALL THE DIFFERENCE ...

Key Learning Points in this chapter

- Why you need a planning 'safety-net'.
- A key question you need to ask every venue - *before* you teach.
- A clever tip on how to deal with an unexpected student
- Why you need to improve your people skills   '
- The importance of keeping in touch with your 'inner beginner'.
- What to do with the student who just *doesn't get it*....
- How to answer that question you don't know the answer to

Until now, we've been working through the positive actions you will need to address before teaching your first class. We've looked at when and where you might teach, creating a lesson plan and how to price your classes. These are all essential steps that, once in place will contribute greatly to you feeling prepared and confident to meet your students.

In this chapter we are going to look at how you can prepare in advance for unexpected situations and problems.

A very experienced teacher once told me that 80% of the effort goes into the planning and preparation stage of a class. So that, on the day, fairly minimal effort – the remaining 20% - is needed to deliver an ace class. She added that, by the end of the class if proper preparation has been observed, the teacher should remain fresh and relaxed and only the students should be tired because they've done all the hard work.

I confess, I rarely feel 'fresh and relaxed' at the end of a class. Leading a group through any kind of creative process is hard work, but I do feel a sort of quiet euphoria and a sense of elation that we all made it through safely to the other side. Maybe this is what she meant...?

So, planning and preparation are the keystones of a successful and enjoyable class - for you and your students. Which is great as long as everything goes smoothly and to plan. But here's the reality and I'm sorry to be the bearer of bad tidings here - even the best prepared for class can fail to go smoothly and completely to plan. In fact, I would go so far as to say that your reputation as a teacher, the respect of your students and your good standing amongst your professional community depends not so much on how you cope when things are going well but how you conduct yourself when they are not.

'I remember one particular student who at the start of the class voiced her disappointment with the programme, saying she'd made all the recipes before. It's important not to let negative comments affect the morale and enthusiasm of other students. Luckily, I found the learner was happy to work to her own schedule so I could concentrate on the other students'. Katie Churchard, Great British Bake Off: The Professionals

Over the years I have been aware of situations where classes have failed due to a minor but unexpected crisis occurring. Occasionally I have even witnessed students being unnecessarily reprimanded or disadvantaged due to adverse situations beyond their control. Nobody wants to feel that personal misfortune or a genuine misunderstanding has led to a classroom crisis.

We're all here to enjoy ourselves and although unexpected situations are well, just that, it is often possible to minimise any adverse impact by - you've got it, more planning!

This second layer of planning is a sort of safety net. An exercise in identifying things that could go wrong and thinking through how the problem or situation could be dealt with or at least, its impact minimised. The good news is that many common sticking points can be managed if you've thought it through beforehand.

Let's look at a few things that could go wrong....

TRAVEL PROBLEMS AND DELAYS

Travel problems can fall into two categories, yours or your students. Let's look at *your* travel plans, first and then the students.

Unless you are lucky enough to be teaching at home, reaching your venue is most likely to involve some element of travel. So, what could go wrong...?

- Significant travel delays or inability to find the venue.

  Make sure you have a telephone number for the venue or a mobile number for a contact who you can warn of a delay or provide further directions.

I'm hoping you will have planned your journey and how to find the venue but occasionally locating either a rural or an inner city address can be a challenge.

When planning journey times calculate for the worst possible trip and aim to arrive at least an hour before the advertised start time.

- Students arriving late due to travel problems

Major travel disruption is rare but seriously adverse weather conditions or motorway closures may require negotiation with your host or venue as to the possibility of delaying start times.

More common is the lone student who arrives late for class. The general rule here must be, as far as possible, to adhere to the timings the rest of the group are expecting. Delaying the start annoys everyone who has arrived on time and unless you can make up the time during the day may mean a later than expected finish which can create even more problems down the line.

UNEXPECTED PROBLEMS AT THE VENUE

I remember arriving at one particular town centre venue to discover there was absolutely no parking available, and also to find that my classroom was on the third floor, with no lift.

This caused so many problems. I had to unload my equipment onto the pavement, whilst partially blocking the high street and then rely upon the venue staff to move my boxes inside whilst I went in search of parking. I don't travel light; there was a lot to shift. It was an extremely stressful start to the day, which could have been avoided if I'd either visited the venue beforehand to check it out, or specifically asked in advance about parking and stairs. I now make a point of doing both and recommend you do the same.

MORE STUDENTS THAN EXPECTED

This always seems like it should be so simple. Question: How many students have booked for my class? Answer: 10 (or insert appropriate number here). Easy peasy, it's just the matter of head count. Unfortunately - not.

For some reason, knowing exactly how many students will arrive is a virtual impossibility.

Of course, there is occasionally someone who unfortunately is unable to attend on the day, and having fewer people than planned for isn't usually a major problem. This can be annoying though, especially if you've invested in materials or equipment for that person to use.

It can be far more problematic if one or two people make a last-minute booking, transfer from another class or for some other reason, arrive in your classroom unexpectedly. Try not to let this throw you and make them welcome.

And always, always, always ensure you have enough handouts, resources and materials for at least one more person than expected.

STUDENTS WITH SPECIAL NEEDS

It is really helpful if either the venue or the student themselves can make you aware in advance of any specific resources or special provision that might be required. Mostly, this does happen but occasionally a communication gets missed and special requests need to be dealt with on the day.

For example, a wheel chair user, a partially sighted participant or someone who's broken a limb since booking - may need to be accommodated at short notice.

In these situations, common sense, quick thinking and being sensitive to both the needs of the individual and the group dynamic need to be applied.

'I occasionally teach large classes where it's not possible to spend as much time with each person as ideally, I would like to. I've found the solution is to make projects as fool proof as possible and to refine both the printed instructions and my presentations so that students can progress on their own'. Jamie Chalmers, Mr X Stitch.

DEALING WITH DIFFICULT PEOPLE ....

In Chapter Two we looked at the personal qualities needed to be a great teacher. We've discovered that you need to be organised, patient and approachable. But my favourite quality, because I think it is absolutely indispensable, is *great people skills*.

Teaching is a people based job. As teachers we are educating, informing, encouraging and inspiring real people. Real people who have paid to learn with us and deserve the best we can give. This wonderful world is full of so many different types of people, confident, shy, happy, sad, the quick to learn and those who find the whole learning experience quite daunting. The greatest skill of the teacher is to bring together these diverse characters and lead them through the creative process in harmony and joy.

Sometimes, 'harmony and joy' can be difficult to achieve. The different characters you'll meet in class can be challenging, demanding and sometimes even downright difficult. So, it's worth putting some thought into how you might deal with them before you meet them.

'I now have a tried and tested set of lesson plans that I know work well and deliver a great class. Photography is all about quick thinking and adapting to the moment so I experience very few problem situations that can't be easily and quickly resolved. Having worked in war zones, avoiding conflict and reacting quickly to changing situations is all part of the job....!' Anthony Cullen, Photographer

CLASSROOM CHARACTERS: A QUICK INTRODUCTION

The shy person

I love to see students chatting and making friends but I know walking into a room full of strangers can be daunting. Here are a few tactics to help students who lack confidence

- Introductions
- Name labels
- Working in pairs
- Sharing tools or equipment
- Extra encouragement & praise

It can also help to sit a quieter student next to a more talkative person...!

The person who wants to make something different.

It still surprises me that even though students sign up for a class that's clearly described as 'beginners' or 'sew a canvas bag' or 'paint a seascape' or 'make a ring', that someone arrives wanting to undertake a completely different project. I used to worry that this only happened to me, that somehow I wasn't being clear on the overall aims and objectives of the class. But as I talk to other creative teachers, it's clear this is more common than you might imagine.

So how we can manage the student who doesn't want to join in with the advertised project?

- Listen very carefully to their reasons for wanting to go off-piste.
- Decide in advance how much leeway you will allow individuals in creating their own project

- Asses if they will be capable of any extra skills needed to be successful
- Do you have sufficient tools or materials to accommodate their request?

But most importantly

- How will having one person working on a different project affect the rest of the group?

I've separated out this last point because in the early days I know I wasn't very good at saying 'no' to student's requests to move away from the advertised programme. I was too keen to keep everyone happy but soon discovered that being nice doesn't always pay.

I found that having one student working independently provokes interest and curiosity from other students and eventually requests to have a go at what the other person is doing.

From here it's a no-win situation;

IF YOU SAY YES - you'll quickly find yourself trying to teach two classes at once.

IF YOU SAY NO - it looks as if you've given preferential treatment to the first person, which then alienates the rest of the class.

It is very, very important to manage the expectations of all students and as far as possible keep everyone working together, to your lesson plan.

So, for the student who really wants to sew a tie, paint a portrait, fashion a tiara or majorly deviate from your lesson plan, be polite but firm. Explain why you are unable to agree to their request and if your class is as brilliant as I know it will be – by the end of the day they will have forgotten and be delighted with what they have made or learned.

'I do occasionally need to temper student's expectations of what they can achieve in class. Sometimes learners arrive with grand ideas to make something that even I would find challenging. Rather than saying a direct no, I usually say that would be hard to achieve in the time allowed but if they really want to try I won't stop them. Mostly by saying this they do change their minds and make something less ambitious. I sometimes mention that they would also need to purchase extra materials which often makes them reconsider...!' Sian Hamilton, editor Making Jewellery magazine

'I'VE BOUGHT A PICTURE OF SOMETHING I WANT TO MAKE'

'I'D LIKE TO MAKE MINE IN A DIFFERENT COLOUR?'

'CAN I MAKE TWO?'

For all of these requests, see the above advice for 'Can I do something different?

The Attention Seeker …..

We know that people sign up for creative classes for many different reasons. Sometimes they need a bit of TLC or little confidence boost.

Unfortunately, this can sometimes come across as attention seeking. A needy student can, unwittingly, be very disruptive in class as they distract you from your lesson plan and more importantly, from your other students. Without a strategy for managing this, other students can start to feel ignored and resentful.

Again, being nice doesn't always pay. Be firm but polite. A friend of mine, who is a very well respected teacher of contemporary flower design, has a brilliant way of doing this, she says.

'I am aware that you are trying to get my attention and I am very happy to help you but there are other people here who equally deserve my time so I'll come back to you just as soon as I can'.

The student who just can't get it!!!

Sometimes, when you become very well practised at what you do, it can be hard to remember what it was like to be a beginner. Actions that seem second nature to you can be perplexing to those doing it for the first time. It's really important, as a teacher, never to lose touch with your 'inner beginner'. If you can still identify with how it felt not to know what comes next, or why a particular stage is so important, it will make you a better teacher.

When I demonstrate a new technique, I often talk about what I was thinking or how I felt when I did it for the first time. I made a lot of mistakes when I first started working with silver clay, simply because I didn't know any better. It helps put beginners at ease if I explain that I was once in their shoes and that I did it wrong, too. Also, students love it if their chosen expert (that's me or you) has a human side, too. Admitting you don't always get it right is one of the best ways to build a good rapport with your class.

So learning a new creative skill can be challenging but what do you do when you've repeated your demo, several times, explained in the simplest words you can find, listened to and answered every possible question but there is still one person in the class who just doesn't get it ?

I'm pleased to say this doesn't happen very often but it's worth having a strategy to deal with it when it does. Firstly, always remember that people - in most cases, don't choose to *not* understand.

They are genuinely confused or in some way unable to process or make sense of the information you are offering. This can be quite intimidating, especially if everyone else seems to be doing well.

So be kind, be patient but recognise that there does come a point when you will need to quietly explain that in order to meet the class objectives or reach a specific time point, you will need to move forward with the rest of the class.

If possible, offer to help during a break, ask the student if they would like to take a shorter lunch so you can work together or offer to email further instructions so the project can be completed at home.

It is so important not to become so sidetracked by your efforts to help one student that the rest of the class suffers.

'One of the most important lessons I've learned is not to focus on negative leaners, just be supportive. Also, wherever possible, make friends with other teachers as their support and experience is invaluable when starting out'. Katie Churchard, Great British Bake Off: the Professionals.

HOW TO ANSWER THE QUESTION YOU DON'T KNOW THE ANSWER TO......

I love it and I mean LOVE it when students ask me a question I don't know the answer to. Why?

Because I learn so much from these questions and I don't just mean that I find out the answer and learn it for next time.

Think of questions asked in class as a kind of barometer of what your students are thinking and how their minds are working.

What may at first appear to be a completely outlandish question could be a sign that the student is actively thinking through every possibility and may see a problem or an opportunity that hasn't occurred to you? What can you learn from this...?

The real beauty of these completely off the wall questions is that they can be used to add interest to future classes. Incorporating them into your dialogue can be amusing, interesting and if one person's mind works in this way, you can be sure that eventually someone else's will too and this time, you'll be ahead of the game.

Unusual questions can often lead to great discussions. I'm very open about admitting that I don't know absolutely everything about my subject so I often open the question out to the class to get their views. Some of the best group conversations start this way.

Above all, be honest if you don't know the answer. If it's a technical or process question seek out the answer and offer to let the student know later. Then, make a note and see what you more you can learn from the question.

'If one student asks a question which I think others might also be interested in, I ring a cow bell to gain everyone's attention and talk the answer through with the whole class. It also means I only need to say it once....!' Louise Talbot, Cutting the Curd Cheese making Classes

ACTION POINTS FROM THIS CHAPTER

- Actively consider which of the above scenarios may occur in your classroom and plan how you might deal with them
- Are there any others not mentioned here?
- Decide how far you are willing to let individuals differ from your lesson plan and how you will politely inform them if their request is not possible.
- Make a checklist of questions to pose to new venues in advance of your class.
- Resolve to put your class first and not to be too 'nice' if it puts your lesson plan at risk.

CHAPTER TEN

The Future

'It is not in the stars to hold our destiny, but in ourselves'

William Shakespeare

WHAT NEXT? HOW TO GROW AND DEVELOP YOUR CREATIVE BUSINESS.

Key learning points in this chapter

- Why now is the time to teach what you do
- The benefits of becoming an expert
- Could a formal qualification be the key to earning more?
- Why you need to make friends with the video button on your mobile phone ...!
- Why I recommend writing a book

Whilst researching and writing this book I've spoken to lots of wonderful creative people who have expanded their skills into teaching what they do.

Their enthusiasm for their subject and passion for teaching have inspired me hugely. Even more heartening is the fact that every single one of them has spoken very positively about the future.

'I see the future as very bright. Globalisation has had its day, the handmade renaissance is very much on the up'. Jamie Chalmers, Mr X Stitch

It seems interest in creative, artisan and handmade skills is very much on the rise. If the future really is handmade, then not only will it feature many more of the creative arts but also more opportunities for creatives to take their future into their own hands and shape it to suit their careers, lifestyle and aspirations.

'The Sewing Bee has had an amazing effect on the sewing world. I feel that the future is bright and both tutors and students want to join in the action!' May Martin, Judge,
The Great British Sewing Bee

What might this mean for you? I hope by now you will be well on the way to teaching what you do but next year or the year after, what will you be doing to take your dream forward?

BECOMING AN EXPERT

Personal development

The phrase, 'personal development' might sound rather corporate or better aligned to more formal careers but what it really means is taking responsibility for your own growth and self-development. How can you progress and nurture your new career as a creative teacher?

One possibility might be to gain formal qualifications either in your subject area or teaching in general.

Formal Qualifications

In Chapter Seven we looked at how becoming a recognised expert in your subject can not only increase your kudos but also boost earning potential.

Well-established teachers evolve into experts over time and with experience and recommendations. Actively undertaking formal training to enhance your career prospects can never be a bad thing.

Most creative professions have a recognised guild or institute who promote education and learning in their field. Gaining a certificate, diploma or masters level qualification is definitely something to shout about, add to your website or mention in your promotional material. It can advance your standing as a proficient teacher and promote confidence in your classes.

Being formally trained in your creative discipline is great but most of those programmes don't include information specific to teaching. So possibly, a course designed around teaching adults, life-long learning or vocational skills would be more informative.

In the UK City & Guilds offer a selection of diploma and certificate level courses aimed at gaining a formal qualification for teaching in the life-long learning sector.

www.cityandguilds.com

'I have a Certificate in Education following an intensive 3 year course in dress and design, pattern cutting, tailoring, soft furnishing, traditional and modern embroidery. I took the City and Guilds qualification to teach adults so that I could teach part time and be at home with my children'. May Martin, Judge, Great British Sewing Bee

EXERCISE:

List any relevant formal qualifications or experience you already have that could be useful evidence of your creative skills or knowledge. How can you use these credentials to promote yourself as a subject expert?

'How do I see the future for teaching creative skills? Ever-popular crafts will always be in demand so the future can be as rosy as you choose to make it. But if your discipline is on the Red List of Endangered Crafts then you must become an advocate as well as a teacher.' Simon Sonsino, Director, Ardington School of Crafts.

Write a Book

Even as it seems the whole world is going paperless and digital, one of the very best ways to be seen as an 'expert' is to have written a good old-fashioned book on your subject.

Writing a book is a huge piece of work that can take months or even years to plan, research and produce. However, once your book is in print it's a permanent and substantial testimony to your knowledge, skill and expertise. Personally, I feel that writing books has been one of the best things I've ever done. I know some students have found me simply because of my books, whereas others have searched me out after buying my books.

I mention my books when I prospect new venues or bid for work. And probably most importantly, I sell books to students who attend my classes.

Much has been written on how to approach publishers, agents and get your work into print, including the increasingly acceptable medium of self-publishing. If you see yourself as an author I would encourage you to read up on the subject and go for it!

Television and Radio

At first, a TV or radio appearance may sound far more professional that you feel at the moment. But keep an eye open for requests from journalists or features in your local press on subjects related to yours. Prepare a press release, email it and follow up.

Even a small appearance can be something to shout about and will promote both your classes and your standing as an expert in your field.

Social media

If you are using your social media accounts for your business, these can be a great way to post photos of your work, behind the scenes or your students work.

Ask questions, answer questions, promote yourself and your knowledge and join in relevant conversations. It takes time, but it is (mostly) free and can help build your reputation as an informed and authoritative teacher.

My last word on becoming an expert must be to say that many of the wonderful teachers I know, do not have any formal qualifications in either their subject or as teachers. Some became teachers by accident – standing in for an absent colleague, for example. Several made a conscious decision to develop teaching as an additional income stream and others responded to insistent requests for tuition from friends and colleagues and found they enjoyed it.

Some are qualified in a related field but many more draw upon decades of experience to create popular and engaging classes and their students love them.

'I feel really positive about the future for teaching creative skills, even in this technologically advanced society, everyone needs a creative outlet. It's good for the soul. Personally I can't find enough time to teach and my classes sell out very quickly which must say something about the number of people looking for a new creative adventure!' Sian Hamilton, Editor, Making Jewellery magazine

THE FUTURE OF LEARNING

So, it's great news for us that the creative revolution is here to stay. Artisan makers and the 'experience over possessions' movement are tapping into the spirit of learning and handmade being better than mass production and consumerism.

'For teachers who can adapt their classes to suit new and exciting trends and adjust content meet the demands of the growing tribe of contemporary learners: I believe the future looks incredibly promising'. Katie Churchard, Bake Off: the Professionals

However, I notice an intriguing contrast between the above sensibilities and how I see the world of learning developing. If you look to the US, the phenomena of online learning is huge. At present, online learning is something we tend to associate with more professional training such as accountancy or law but in the US you can learn almost anything from your tablet, computer or iPhone.

There are a number of enormously popular US based websites who specialise in online video classes teaching creative skills from photography to song writing and graphic design. Some of these sites are filming and producing the classes from their own studios but many are simply hosting video classes created by the makers themselves.

In these instances, the web company issue advice and guidelines around video production and classes are filmed by individuals sometimes as simply as with a mobile phone.

The concept may seem astonishing to us at the moment but the reality is it opens up a worldwide audience with 24/7 access to your teaching.

"The internet and social media have democratised learning and creative inspiration. It's now easier than ever to meander down a creative pathway and find real joy in simple, handmade crafts'. Jamie Chalmers, Mr X Stitch

Clearly, this is not for the camera-shy or technologically challenged and I put my own hand up here - but maybe it is a wake-up call to the fact that the world of learning and teaching is changing fast and now may be the time to start honing those video skills or get left behind...?

The same applies to...

WEBINARS

A webinar is an online presentation that happens in real-time. The presenter uses a webcam to film his or herself talking, making or presenting to an online audience who can be worldwide. Webinars are already being used as an effective teaching tool and can be a great way to meet a new tech-savvy audience.

SOCIAL MEDIA – LIVE!

Both Facebook and Instagram now have features that enable us to broadcast live video and sound directly to our friends, fans and followers. Because it's so new, those platforms are super-keen for us show-off their new features and so prioritise this type of content.

It's another no cost way to reach your audience and build your reputation as a teacher so figure out those video controls and be brave!

'The future – I see the future for teaching creative skills as being very positive. There's a great enthusiasm for knowledge right now that we can all tap into'.
Anthony Cullen, Photographer

ACTION POINTS FROM THIS CHAPTER

- Positivity for the future. You are in the right place at exactly the right time and this is just the start of an amazing journey
- What personal development might you need now or plan for in the future to help you learn and grow in your new role?
- Think about how you might be able to use emerging technologies to reach new audiences
- Keep moving forward

PARTING ADVICE

Teaching what you do is an adventure. Not only will you be continuing to use your skills and talents in your craft but deciding how you design and develop your classes is a creative process, too. And don't forget, if you're not ready to quit your day job just yet, building your very own 'side-hustle' could be the perfect solution.

However...

If we are all honest, there is sometimes this tiny voice of doubt in our heads asking 'what will I do if it doesn't work out'.

And whilst I wholeheartedly encourage you to try teaching what you do, I also urge you to be prepared to change and adapt as you develop your new career. By reading this book, I know you will be much better prepared to plan, promote and run your own classes, than I was. But it is foolish to imagine that we know it all and only our way will succeed.

However perfect your lesson plan it is vain to assume that this is exactly what will work for every student who ever comes to your classes.

Looking back, the biggest challenges and the biggest changes I've faced during my own teaching journey came from situations and problems I could not have anticipated at the beginning. If I'd have stuck to my guns about every decision I made in the early days I probably wouldn't be writing this book now.

The fact that some of my big ideas either didn't prove to be popular or just didn't work out, has given me a kind of quiet confidence that even if I don't know all the answers right now, I know enough to get started and then adapt and change as things become clearer.

So, what have I learned from the things that didn't work out

• Don't waste too much energy making every single element of your plan 100% perfect before making a start. It causes delay and it's most likely numerous elements will need to be fine-tuned or adjusted as you go along.

• Listen and get feedback. Talk to your customers at every opportunity. Ask for their thoughts and comments about you, your classes, everything!

• Keep fine-tuning. Nothing is set in stone or ever finished. Change, adapt and do it again.

As someone said, the greatest barrier to success is getting started.

You've made a great start by buying this book.

Now read it, do the exercises and get started.

I know you're going to be a great teacher.

Melanie x

Teach What You Do – Contributors

My most enormous thanks to every one of the amazing teachers who have so kindly contributed their thoughts and ideas for this book.

Most of you I have the pleasure of knowing personally and many of you are friends as well as classroom colleagues. All of you have inspired me with your knowledge, your professionalism and your endless enthusiasm for your subjects.

Your support and sense of humour have encouraged me in continuing my own journey as a teacher and in writing this book.

Thank you x

Jamie Chalmers – Mr X Stitch

Jamie Chalmers, aka Mr X Stitch, aka the Kingpin of Contemporary Embroidery, took up cross stitching fifteen years ago and he's never looked back.

Since establishing the Mr X Stitch website in 2008, he has been showcasing new talent in the world of textiles and stitch and has curated a number of stitch-based exhibitions in the UK and Ireland. Jamie is an accomplished and internationally exhibited artist in his own right, the curator of PUSH Stitchery and the author of the 'Mr X Stitch Guide to Cross Stitch'. He is the founder of the game-changing XStitch cross stitch design magazine which launched in summer 2017.

Jamie is an active leader in the online stitch community and what he has dubbed 'the new embroidery movement' and is active on various social networking platforms. He loves introducing new people to the benefits of embroidery from a creative and wellbeing standpoint and is proud to be an ambassador for this ubiquitous craft.

https://www.youtube.com/c/MrXStitch

Facebook @mrxstitch

Instagram @mrxstitch

Katie Churchard

One half of the formidable team representing the WI Cookery School for Channel 4's Bake Off: The Professionals. With almost twenty years of experience, Katie is an expert in Patisserie and Confectionery having worked her culinary magic at both The Mandarin Oriental Hotel, London and Le Manoir Aux Quat Saison, Oxford.

Since gaining Level 5 Diploma in Education and Training, Katie has become a respected teacher and trainer specialising in baking, chocolate and patisserie. She is also a regular guest tutor at the WI Cookery School.

Katie is currently Chef Instructor for Cambridge Regional College.

Twitter @katiechurchard

Anthony Cullen

Anthony Cullen is an Observer award winning photographer with over 25 years' experience. He regularly shoots international and national editorial features and advertising campaigns for clients including Adnams, The Sunday Times and Land Rover. His base is in Suffolk at the beautiful Pin Mill Studio on the banks of the River Orwell. For the past seven years Anthony has run group and individual classes alongside his day job.

www.photographicday.com

www.anthonycullen.com

Facebook @anthonycullenphotography

Instagram @anthonycullenphotography

Sian Hamilton

Sian Hamilton is a freelance jewellery teacher, editor, author and web designer in the UK. She has a BA in 3D Design specialising in silver and ceramics and has been in the design industry for over 25 years. Sian is the Editor of Making Jewellery magazine in the UK and in recent years has written 8 'how to' jewellery and craft books. She started teaching silver clay classes in 2017 and now teaches every week, mostly in the evenings to work around all the other contracts she has!

www.hamiltonjewellery.com

Facebook @sianleeperhamilton

May Martin

Star of the Great British Sewing Bee and doyenne of the Women's Institute, May Martin has been teaching sewing for over 40 years. She is an extraordinarily experienced teacher with a career that has been both exciting and interesting with tremendous variety, from running a needlework department to undertaking commissions for textile refurbishment of complete houses. She enjoys giving talks & demonstrations around the country and was recently a judge on The Great British Sewing Bee, for the BBC.

Her best-selling book 'May Martin's Sewing Bible: 40 years of tips and tricks', was published in 2014. May has a real passion for her subject and still enjoys sharing her skills and inspiring others. She can be found teaching at Denman College in Oxfordshire.

Louise Talbot

Qualified teacher Louise Talbot has been making cheese for almost twenty years and combines her passion with teaching others, at her 'Cutting the Curd' Cheese Making Classes.

Louise is a member of the Specialist Cheese Makers Association and The Guild of Fine Foods and guest tutor at many Cookery Schools, including Waitrose, Leith's School of Food and Wine, Divertimenti and WI Denman College and is also a World Cheese Awards, Global Cheese Awards and Great Taste judge.

www.cuttingthecurd.co.uk

Facebook @cuttingthecurdcheesemakingclasses

Simon Sonsino

Simon Sonsino is a British calligrapher, textual artist and international selling author who specialises in abstract expressionist art using calligraphy and all aspects of letterform. Director of Ardington School of Crafts in Oxfordshire, where Simon teaches his own classes as well as co-ordinating the work of many other experienced creative teachers. These different roles give Simon a unique insight to the opportunities for teaching contemporary art and craft skills in the UK today.

Always looking to enhance his art and evolve his style by researching different media in which to include letterform such as clay, textiles and stained glass. Simon is also the author of 'Textual Art: Inspiration and techniques for Creating Art with Calligraphy'.

www.simonsonsino.com

www.ardingtonschool.com

And, lastly, with very special thanks to my assistant and sister, Karen Blake, whose help and advice has been invaluable in both teaching my classes and writing this book. Thank you for all your hard work, patience, good ideas and spreadsheets without which 'Teach What You Do' would not have happened.

Thank you!

Mx

About the Author

Melanie Blaikie has been teaching contemporary silver-smithing and creative jewellery skills since 2003. She is one of the UK's foremost teachers in the medium of clay silver and is in demand at colleges, craft schools and other prestigious venues across the UK and abroad.

Her sell-out classes introduce beginners and experts alike to new ideas, innovative techniques and endless creative possibilities. Students praise her calm and positive approach, always encouraging and inspiring leaners to achieve more than expected.

Melanie is an internationally selling author, her book 'Silver Clay Workshop: a complete guide to getting started with silver clay jewellery', is the definitive guide to working with this innovative medium.

As well as writing and contributing to numerous other publications and creative press, Melanie also mentors new teachers and speaks on creative subjects around the UK.

www.melanieblaikie.com

Facebook @melanieblaikie
Instagram @melanie_blaikie
Twitter   @melanieblaikie

NOTES

NOTES

NOTES

NOTES

Printed in Great Britain
by Amazon